P9-ARR-667

SOPHOCLES

Electra

Translated by
ANNE CARSON
With Introduction and Notes by
MICHAEL SHAW

OXFORD
UNIVERSITY PRESS

2001

OXFORD
UNIVERSITY PRESS

Oxford   New York
Athens   Auckland   Bangkok   Bogotá   Buenos Aires   Calcutta
Cape Town   Chennai   Dar es Salaam   Delhi   Florence   Hong Kong   Istanbul
Karachi   Kuala Lumpur   Madrid   Melbourne   Mexico City   Mumbai
Nairobi   Paris   São Paulo   Shanghai   Singapore   Taipei   Tokyo   Toronto   Warsaw

and associated companies in
Berlin   Ibadan

Copyright © 2001 by Anne Carson and Michael Shaw

Published by Oxford University Press, Inc.
198 Madison Avenue, New York, New York 10016

Oxford is a registered trademark of Oxford University Press

All rights reserved. No part of this publication may be reproduced,
stored in a retrieval system, or transmitted, in any form or by any means,
electronic, mechanical, photocopying, recording, or otherwise,
without the prior permission of Oxford University Press.

Library of Congress Cataloging-in-Publication Data
Sophocles.
[Electra. English]
Electra / Sophocles: translated by Anne Carson, with introduction and notes by Michael
Shaw.
p.   cm. — (The Greek tragedy in new translations)
ISBN 0-19-504960-8 (pbk.)
1. Electra (Greek mythology) — Drama.   I. Carson, Anne, 1950–   II. Shaw,
Michael.   III. Title.   IV. Series.
PA4414.E5C37   2001
882'.01—dc21

00-033971

9 8 7 6 5 4 3 2 1
Printed in the United States of America

HOUSTON PUBLIC LIBRARY

R01211 93986

THE GREEK TRAGEDY
IN NEW TRANSLATIONS

GENERAL EDITORS
Peter Burian and Alan Shapiro

SOPHOCLES: Electra

EDITORS' FOREWORD

"*The Greek Tragedy in New Translations* is based on the conviction that poets like Aeschylus, Sophocles, and Euripides can only be properly rendered by translators who are themselves poets. Scholars may, it is true, produce useful and perceptive versions. But our most urgent present need is for a *re-creation* of these plays—as though they had been written, freshly and greatly, by masters fully at home in the English of our own times."

With these words, the late William Arrowsmith announced the purpose of this series, and we intend to honor that purpose. As was true of most of the volumes that began to appear in the 1970s—first under Arrowsmith's editorship, later in association with Herbert Golder—those for which we bear editorial responsibility are products of close collaboration between poets and scholars. We believe (as Arrowsmith did) that the skills of both are required for the difficult and delicate task of transplanting these magnificent specimens of another culture into the soil of our own place and time, to do justice both to their deep differences from our patterns of thought and expression and to their palpable closeness to our most intimate concerns. Above all, we are eager to offer contemporary readers dramatic poems that convey as vividly and directly as possible the splendor of language, the complexity of image and idea, and the intensity of emotion of the originals. This entails, among much else, the recognition that the tragedies were meant for performance—as scripts for actors—to be sung and danced as well as spoken. It demands writing of inventiveness, clarity, musicality, and dramatic power. By such standards we ask that these translations be judged.

This series is also distinguished by its recognition of the need of nonspecialist readers for a critical introduction informed by the best recent scholarship, but written clearly and without condescension.

Each play is followed by notes designed not only to elucidate obscure references but also to mediate the conventions of the Athenian stage as well as those features of the Greek text that might otherwise go unnoticed. The notes are supplemented by a glossary of mythical and geographical terms that should make it possible to read the play without turning elsewhere for basic information. Stage directions are sufficiently ample to aid readers in imagining the action as they read. Our fondest hope, of course, is that these versions will be staged not only in the minds of their readers but also in the theaters to which, after so many centuries, they still belong.

A NOTE ON THE SERIES FORMAT

A series such as this requires a consistent format. Different translators, with individual voices and approaches to the material in hand, cannot be expected to develop a single coherent style for each of the three tragedians, much less make clear to modern readers that, despite the differences among the tragedians themselves, the plays share many conventions and a generic, or period, style. But they can at least share a common format and provide similar forms of guidance to the reader.

1. *Spelling of Greek names*

Orthography is one area of difference among the translations that requires a brief explanation. Historically, it has been common practice to use Latinized forms of Greek names when bringing them into English. Thus, for example, Oedipus (not Oidipous) and Clytemnestra (not Klutaimestra) are customary in English. Recently, however, many translators have moved toward more precise transliteration, which has the advantage of presenting the names as both Greek and new, instead of Roman and neoclassical importations into English. In the case of so familiar a name as Oedipus, however, transliteration risks the appearance of pedantry or affectation. And in any case, perfect consistency cannot be expected in such matters. Readers will feel the same discomfort with "Athenai" as the chief city of Greece as they would with "Platon" as the author of the *Republic*.

The earlier volumes in this series adopted as a rule a "mixed" orthography in accordance with the considerations outlined above. The most familiar names retain their Latinate forms, the rest are transliterated; –os rather than Latin –us is adopted for the termination of masculine names, and Greek diphthongs (such as Iphigene*ia* for Latin Iphigenia) are retained. Some of the later volumes continue this practice, but where translators have preferred to use a more consistent practice of transliteration or Latinization, we have honored their wishes.

2. Stage directions

The ancient manuscripts of the Greek plays do not supply stage directions (though the ancient commentators often provide information rel-
evant to staging, delivery, "blocking," etc.). Hence stage directions must
be inferred from words and situations and our knowledge of Greek
theatrical conventions. At best this is a ticklish and uncertain procedure. But it is surely preferable that good stage directions should be
provided by the translator than that readers should be left to their own
devices in visualizing action, gesture, and spectacle. Ancient tragedy
was austere and "distanced" by means of masks, which means that the
reader must not expect the detailed intimacy ("He shrugs and turns
wearily away," "She speaks with deliberate slowness, as though to em-
phasize the point," etc.) that characterizes stage directions in modern
naturalistic drama.

3. Numbering of lines

For the convenience of the reader who may wish to check the English
against the Greek text or vice versa, the lines have been numbered
according to both the Greek text and the translation. The lines of the
English translation have been numbered in multiples of ten, and these
numbers have been set in the right-hand margin. The notes that follow
the text have been keyed to the line numbers of the translation. The
(inclusive) Greek numeration will be found bracketed at the top of the
page. Readers will doubtless note that in many plays the English lines
outnumber the Greek, but they should not therefore conclude that the
translator has been unduly prolix. In most cases the reason is simply
that the translator has adopted the free-flowing norms of modern Anglo-
American prosody, with its brief-breath- and emphasis-determined
lines, and its habit of indicating cadence and caesuras by line length
and setting rather than by conventional punctuation. Other translators
have preferred to cast dialogue in more regular five-beat or six-beat
lines, and in these cases Greek and English numerations will tend to
converge.

Durham, N.C.   PETER BURIAN
Chapel Hill, N.C.   ALAN SHAPIRO
2000

CONTENTS

ELECTRA

INTRODUCTION

The long siege of Troy, a city on the coast of Asia Minor, is one of the major events in the world of Greek myth. The first surviving work of Greek literature, the *Iliad* of Homer, is largely concerned with it. The *Iliad* itself is about an event in the ninth year of that siege, a quarrel in the Greek camp between Agamemnon, the leader of the Greek rulers, and Achilles, their best warrior, that leads to Achilles' withdrawal. This in turn leads to a series of events that end with the death of the Trojans' best warrior, Hector. But in the course of that story, Homer tells us much of the earlier history of the war and reveals that after Hector's death Troy's fall will inevitably follow.

Homer's *Odyssey* is concerned with the ten years' wandering and eventual return home of Odysseus, another Greek leader at Troy. Here, too, other stories are brought in, among them the story of Agamemnon's return home and his murder by Aegisthus and his wife. While he had been in Troy, his cousin Aegisthus had seduced his wife, Clytemnestra, and upon his return home Aegisthus and Clytemnestra had arranged a feast for him at which he, his war-prize and concubine Cassandra, and his followers were murdered. Eight years later, Orestes, his son, returned to Mycenae and murdered Aegisthus and buried Aegisthus and Clytemnestra—Homer does not say who killed her. In the references to this event, Orestes' action is always viewed in a positive light—he is pointed out as an example for Odysseus' son Telemachus to follow, as he comes of age, and becomes dissatisfied with the suitors of his mother who have made themselves at home for several years and are consuming his estate.

The story of Agamemnon's return is much more elaborate in Aeschylus' dramatic trilogy, the *Oresteia*, which was produced some 250 years later (assuming Homer's date to be about 700 B.C.) in 458 B.C. In particular, the story has become much more problematic. In the first play, the *Agamemnon*, Clytemnestra has been given a new and powerful motive for killing her husband: his sacrifice of their daughter Iphigenia to Artemis so the Greeks could have fair winds for the voyage to Troy. When Orestes arrives in Argos in the second play, *Libation Bearers*, he is greeted by his sister Electra who has long been praying for his return. She, like Iphigenia, is not mentioned by Homer. Electra bears witness to the scandal and welcomes Orestes, but she does not participate in the murder. In the final play, *Eumenides*, Orestes is pursued by his mother's avenging spirits, stands trial in Athens, and is acquitted, even though by a split decision. Although there are other episodes and variants found in other works, Aeschylus' trilogy is a fair representative of the model Euripides and Sophocles used when they created their two very different plays.

Euripides' *Electra* follows the conventional plot to a degree. Electra bears witness to her mother's crimes and she welcomes Orestes to Argos as avenger, but Euripides shows what the strain of her situation has done to her character. In his version, she has been removed from the palace by her mother and married to a poor but noble farmer in an outlying farm. Her witness-bearing occurs in a context where it is irrelevant, and this, too, has helped to bend her character. She has become obsessive, sexually confused (both repressed and prurient), and, most important, she is unaware of the consequences of murdering her mother. As Clytemnestra approaches, Orestes loses his nerve (or gains his sanity), but Electra forces him to persevere—a vivid dramatization of the force that works through her. However, once they have murdered Clytemnestra, Electra then becomes as extreme in her regret as she was in her vengefulness. She insists the fault is hers and not Orestes'. In the final scene, Euripides states, through a divine spokesman, that the murder was just, that it was wrong that Electra and Orestes should have done it, and also that Apollo is responsible. In other words, the cost of enacting justice is prohibitively high—in this case, it has destroyed Electra and Orestes.

Like Euripides, Sophocles focuses on the relationship between situation and character, but the character of Euripides' Electra is destroyed by her situation, while Sophocles' character resists. She admits that her actions are shameful in themselves, even though they are just, and thus she displays a self-consciousness that is completely lacking in Euripides' Electra. As she puts it, in order to do things that are right, she must do things that are wrong, and her only defense is that she has been forced.

This is a highly satisfactory vengeance drama. Sophocles emphasizes the pathetic aspects of Electra's situation: All the supports she has are gradually removed in the course of the play. Her sister chooses expedient silence; her mother threatens her with force; finally, her main support—the hope that her brother will return—is taken away when his death is falsely reported as part of his vengeance plot. Only then, when she is betrayed, alone, and completely lacking in hope, Orestes reveals himself to her. The play then wheels from noble suffering to vindication. Electra indulges herself in extreme joy at her brother's return, and her pleasure at the death of Clytemnestra and Aegisthus is grim but not excessive.

Those elements of the story that would destroy this effect have been dampened. Electra's antagonists display unprincipled expediency and violence. It is clear that Electra should prevail; since we the audience know that Orestes has arrived, we are certain that she will prevail. Once Orestes sets his plot in motion, he dispatches his mother quickly and after minimal verbal sparring he leads Aegisthus into the house to be killed in a manner we are not allowed to contemplate.

It is not hard to see why some have concluded that it is primarily a play of revenge. However, it is difficult to believe that our response should be so uncomplicated. Orestes' murder of his mother is monstrous behavior. This difficulty has to a great degree been suppressed in Sophocles' play. It is not repressed in Aeschylus' trilogy, and Orestes himself understands that what he is doing is monstrous: "I have been made into a snake in order to kill her." This monstrousness, externalized and personified as the Furies, threatens to destroy him. When Orestes and Apollo argue against the Furies in the law court setting of the third play of this trilogy, we see how closely balanced the arguments for and against the murder are, and how national interest, the highest of motives, only carries the day by the slimmest margin.

Although it is generally felt that Sophocles' Electra is an admirable person and that the revenge is necessary, it is possible to draw the conclusion that she and Orestes are driven by motives that they do not understand to perform an action of which no one—not even Apollo—approves, and that Electra becomes insane in the course of the play.[1] This dark reading is based on a relatively small number of passages. Electra undercuts her own position when she makes the point to Clytemnestra that vengeance leads to endless retaliation. Clytemnestra reveals that

---

1. See Sophocles, *Electra*, edited by J. H. Kells, Cambridge University Press, 1973, pp. 8–11, for the strongest version known to me of the dark reading, which he calls the ironic theory, basing his discussion on the two articles by J. T. Sheppard cited below. This discussion by Kells is the basis for this paragraph. C. P. Segal, *Tragedy and Civilization: An Interpretation of Sophocles* ("Martin Classical Lectures," vol. 26), Cambridge and London: Harvard University Press, 1981, discusses the "darker view," which he agrees with, in his chapter on *Electra* pp. 249–91.

she has some maternal feelings for her son after hearing the account of his death. After Orestes reveals himself to her, Electra, who has devoted herself so absolutely to justice, makes several disturbingly opportunistic remarks. She agrees to deceive Clytemnestra so she can be true to "the good luck that now attends us,"[2] and later says (ironically) to Aegisthus that "I've learned to side with the winners" (1928). Electra becomes increasingly out of touch with reality as the play progresses—first planning to kill Aegisthus herself, and later thinking that the Old Man is her father. Finally, she refuses to let Aegisthus speak in his own defense because she wants "satisfaction for her wounded feelings."[3]

In this reading, Sophocles' Electra is a near double of the Euripidean Electra. But it is possible to account for these passages and to come to less extreme conclusions about Electra's mental state. Sheppard suggests that Electra acts like a sane and moral person most of the time, but occasionally we see "hints of the chaos ruling in those tragic souls."[4] Thus, to respond to the dark reading it is necessary to consider not only the meaning of these passages but also the way they fit into the play's full context.[5]

The play begins in a manner that suggests it will follow the same course taken by Aeschylus in the Libation Bearers. Orestes enters with the Old Man, his former tutor, and says that he inquired of Apollo at Delphi how to exact justice from the murderers and that the god gave this answer:

> *Take no weapons.*
> *No shield.*
> *No army.*
> *Go alone—a hand in the night.*
> *Snare them.*
> *Slaughter them.*
> *You have the right.* (46–52)

---

2. Kells' translation of line 1306, line 1740 in this translation. Our translation has "the god who stands beside us now," but a more literal translation says "the present *daimon.*" A *daimon* is indeed a divinity, but in phrases like the one here the word only means "the spirit of the moment."

3. Kells, p. 11.

4. J. T. Sheppard, "*Electra* Again." *Classical Review* 41 (1927) 165. This and the two other articles by Sheppard concerning *Electra* remain among the most interesting treatments of this play: "The Tragedy of Electra, According to Sophocles." *Classical Quarterly* 12 (1918) 80–88; "Electra: A Defense of Sophocles." *Classical Review* 41 (1927) 2–9.

5. I have omitted one major claim of the dark reading, that Orestes asked the wrong question of the oracle, for reasons discussed in C. M. Bowra, *Sophoclean Tragedy*, Oxford: Clarendon Press, 1944, pp. 215–18. In brief, although Orestes failed to ask the oracle if he should murder his mother, the oracular response was not ambiguous, doubts are not raised elsewhere in the play, and the project seems here as in Aeschylus to have divine favor.

In this version, Apollo's oracle did not say why a trick was necessary. In the Aeschylean version, on the other hand, the oracle told Orestes to pursue his father's murderers "in the same fashion, death for death" (*Libation Bearers*, 273–74). When Aeschylus' Orestes refers to the trick, it is clear that he knows why a trick is necessary:

> You must hide what we have discussed here,
> so that those who killed a respected man with
>   a trick
> might be taken with a trick, dying in the self-
>   same noose,
> the way Loxias proclaimed,
> He who is Lord, Apollo, true prophet from of
>   old.   (*Libation Bearers*, 555–59)

Sophocles' Orestes does not have the benefit of this explanation, and he is uneasy about lying about his own death. His explanation is less than adequate:

> Can a mere story be evil? No of course not—
> so long as it pays in the end.   (85–86)

This is the cheap language of politics. The lie he has chosen, a chariot wreck at Delphi, reflects the limited perspective of a rich teenager of his times. In the midst of this pedestrian stuff he can suddenly inject language of a much higher level, "I come to cleanse you with justice" (97). But on the whole Sophocles' Orestes is a typical person of his age and class, who only partly understands what he has undertaken.

For the most part, this scene has been prosaic, and there is a sharp contrast with Electra's first word. A cry is heard from offstage—"O wretched me" is a close translation of *moi dystenos*—and Orestes immediately echoes that word, "Can it be *poor* (*dystenos*) Electra? Should we stay here and listen?" (111). The Old Man seems to drag him away: "No. Nothing precedes the work of Apollo."

After the men leave, Electra enters. Perhaps she is in rags, but it is more likely that she is in the plain dress of a servant.[6] Her language continues to be highly emotional:

6. What is she wearing? The text does not give us much help on this point. In line 257 of this translation she says she is in "rags" but a closer translation is "unseemly dress" (line 193 in the Greek). Orestes asks, "It shocks me, the way you look: do they abuse you? (1181)" In a melodrama of this intensity, whether Electra is dressed as a commoner or is in rags is an important issue. My own feeling is that to dress her in rags would be too extreme. J. C. Kamerbeek implies that Electra

> O holy light!
> And equal air shaped on the world—
> you hear my songs,
> you hear the blows fall. (115–18)

It is as though the scene has suddenly shifted from black and white to color. She is singing, for one thing. She does not speak about things so much as she speaks to them, a mark of heightened emotion—she addresses the light, the air, her father, Hades, Persephone. She turns quickly to her father's murder:

> No pity for these things,
> there is no pity
> but mine,
> oh father,
> for the pity of your butchering rawblood death. (133–37)

We do not stop to think about it, but Orestes said nothing of how he feels about his father.

After Electra's speech ends, there is a lyric dialogue (*kommos*) between Electra and the chorus. The tension between them is visible from the beginning:

> Your mother is evil
> but oh my child why
> melt your life away in mourning? (163–65)

Choruses are typically suspicious of extreme behavior. Already the words characteristic of the Sophoclean hero have begun to appear.[7]

has been doing harm to herself after hearing of Orestes' death, and if this is so it must occur on stage (*The Electra*, Leiden: Brill, 1974, note on 1177). This seems likely—in the rehearsals for the Kansas University student production that I attended in 1978, it was decided that she should roll on the ground during the messenger speech. It is also possible that she causes herself harm in a later scene. She announces that she is lying down at 819, and she may roll on the ground and lacerate herself in the *kommos*, 823–70, since such gestures are often referred to in similar passages in tragedy, although not here. The director, Bill Nesbitt, graciously allowed me to attend all aspects of this production, beginning with the auditions and ending with the faculty oral evaluation of the director. My reading of this play and my approach to Greek drama in general has been deeply influenced by this experience. I am especially indebted to Mr. Nesbitt, to Kathleen Warfel, who played Electra, and to Professors Ron Willis and Jack Wright.

7. This aspect of the Sophoclean hero was brilliantly delineated by Bernard Knox in *The Heroic Temper: Studies in Sophoclean Tragedy*, Berkeley: University of California Press, 1964.

Electra calls on Philomela (199) and Niobe (202), both of whom lament "endlessly" (*aien*, a word associated with Sophoclean heroes). The chorus say "you go too far" (209). The chorus urge her to find a middle ground between hating and forgetting (237–38). They inform her that she "must not clash / with the people in power" (293–94). It sounds as if Sophocles' earlier *Antigone* is being played out again, and we will hear more echoes of that play, particularly in the dialogues of Electra and her sister.

However, what happens next does not have a parallel in *Antigone*. Electra does not answer the chorus' remark in quite the way we expect of Sophoclean heroes:

> I am forced. I know that.
> I see the trap closing.
> I know what I am.
> But while life is in me
> I will not stop this violence. No.   (295–99)

Sophoclean heroes often say that they "must" do something But the implication here is that Electra herself does not fully approve of what she is doing. A nuance in the Greek text, not found in this translation, adds to this impression. A close translation of line 296 ("I see the trap closing") would read, "my anger [*orga*] does not escape me." This self-awareness is unusual for a Sophoclean hero, and it also contrasts with the mood of the female avengers in the dramas by the other playwrights on this theme. Aeschylus' Clytemnestra only becomes aware that some sort of spirit has possessed her after the murder of Agamemnon. Euripides' Electra achieves a similar self-awareness, but only after she has participated in the murder of Clytemnestra.

Electra and the chorus have been singing since she entered, the longest unbroken passage in lyric in Sophocles. She now shifts to iambics, that is, to something more like normal speech. And as often happens in tragedy, she reiterates the gist of what she has been saying in song. She begins with a word that is very important to her:

> Women, I am ashamed before you: I know
> you find me extreme
> in my grief.   (338–40)

Shame is normally considered to be an enforcer of social conformity, but shame makes Electra a rebel. She imagines another person, like herself, doing just as she is doing:

> But how could I—
> how could a woman of any nobility
> stand
> and watch her father's house go bad?
>
> (344–47)

These words suggest that she is not excessively self-absorbed. This "woman of any nobility" is partly a projection of herself, and partly another person; so she attempts to align herself with her society, although it is the aspect of society that reflects her own values.[8] This emphasis on gazing continues:

> I see my father's throne
> with Aegisthus on it.   (358–59)

This early in the play, we have already seen one of the most important aspects of Electra's character, her interest in shame, good conduct, proper religious practice.

Electra also raises another issue that will be important later. Is there any pragmatic justification for her behavior, or is she dangerously out of touch with reality? One answer to this question is that Electra functions as a Fury, and this speech contains the first of two hints that she does. Her mother, she says, "lives with that polluted object, / fearing no Fury"(370–71). Yet when her mother hears that Orestes is coming, she is clearly not so unaffected as Electra has said:

> Then she goes wild, comes screaming at me:
> "Have I you to thank for this?
> Isn't it your work?"   (399–401)

Driving someone "wild" (emmanes) would seem to be an appropriate action for a Fury.[9] Although the threat comes from Orestes, Clytemnestra sees Electra's hand behind Orestes.

Furies are important characters throughout the Oresteia of Aeschylus, and in the final play in that trilogy, the Eumenides, they form the chorus. They define themselves as the avengers of crimes of blood.[10]

---

8. This woman is not quite the same as the "imagined other," whom Bernard Williams discusses in Shame and Necessity, Berkeley: University of California Press, 1993, 82. However, she serves a similar mediating function.

9. See the chorus' description of Clytemnestra in Aeschylus' Agamemnon, line 1428: "her mind is raging [epimainetai] because of the bloody action."

10. Eumenides, 312–20.

One of the ways that they answer the prayers of those unjustly murdered is to drive the guilty person out of his mind.[11] Clytemnestra herself will imply that Electra is a Fury, and at least one scholar sees this as the key to her character, a view that must be at least partially true.[12]

Chrysothemis, Electra's sister, enters when Electra ends her monologue. The contrast between her relatively fine dress and the plainer dress of Electra makes a dramatic point that will be raised in their conversation. She carries offerings in her hands, and clearly she is being diverted from some action to speak to Electra. In her opening words, she reveals that they have had this discussion before:

> Here you are again at the doorway, sister,
> telling your story to the world!
> When will you learn? (444–46)

What Electra has not learned is that she should not indulge her emotions when she can have no effect on the situation. This is essentially what Ismene said to Antigone, the first signal that the scenes between the two sisters will be an elaboration of the conflict of sisters in the *Antigone*.

The chorus has emphasized at Chrysothemis' entrance that she is just like her sister, but there is something that distinguishes them, and Chrysothemis reveals it immediately:

> Yes I know how bad things are.
> I suffer too—if I had the strength
> I would show what I think of them.
>
> (448–50)

What differentiates the two sisters is found in that phrase, "if I had the strength [*sthenos*]." Electra is offended by this remark and throws the word back at her (*sthenos*, 471). The prudential Chrysothemis does not act when she knows she will not succeed:

> Why pretend to be doing,
> unless I can do some real harm? (453–54)

---

11. Ibid., 318–33.
12. See R. P. Winnington-Ingram, *Sophocles: An Interpretation*, Cambridge; New York: Cambridge University Press, 1980, pp. 217–47.

Sophoclean heroes, on the other hand, often say something like this: "I will be stopped if I don't have the strength" (*sthenei; Antigone,* 91). That is, these characters are demonstrating in their quarrels the quality later to be known as *will.*

Chrysothemis continues with an even more revealing remark:

> And yet,
> it is true,
> justice is not on my side.
> Your choice is the right one. On the other hand,
> if I want to live a free woman,
> there are masters who must be obeyed.
>
> (456–61)

Chrysothemis uses a word for justice (*to dikaion*) that is frequently employed in contemporary discussion, as is the phrase she uses, "masters who must be obeyed."[13] In Athenian rhetoric of this period, matters would typically be considered in terms of justice and then in terms of the expedient.[14] The expedient can conveniently be defined as what works. In Sophoclean drama, this expediency language is usually found in the context of moral relativism, as in this remark made by Odysseus in Sophocles' *Philoctetes:*

> As the occasion
> demands, such a one am I.
> When there is a competition of men just and
> good,

---

13. See Kells, note on line 1465, who refers to Thrasymachus' statement in Plato's *Republic* that justice is "going along with the stronger." The usual term for this concept is expedience (*to sympheron*). Although Chrysothemis does not use it here, Electra uses one form of this word in 1465 ("to *side with* [*sympherein*] the winners"). There is an extensive discussion of expediency argument in W. K. C. Guthrie, *The Sophists* (Vol. 3, Pt. 1, *A History of Greek Philosophy*), Cambridge: 1971, pp. 84–116.

14. The expedient is discussed with respect to Thucydides in Colin Macleod's article, "Form and Meaning in the Melian Dialogue," in *Collected Essays,* Oxford: Clarendon Press; New York: Oxford University Press, 1983, 52–67. This remark is as true of tragedy as it is of Thucydides, "Now justice and expediency are what in rhetorical terms are called *telika kephalaia,* qualities human action should aim to have. Rhetoricians often fuse them together, ... to make the course the speaker advises or defends appear satisfactory from as many points of view as possible. ... But, as is well known, it is particularly characteristic of Thucydides to contrapose the two" (p. 55). I am indebted to Macleod's essays in various ways in this essay.

you will find none more scrupulous than
myself.
What I seek in everything is to win . . . [15]

The ironic usage of "free woman" in Chrysothemis' lines should not
be passed by without notice. Normally those who obey masters are
slaves. Chrysothemis is defining "free" in terms of expedience—that
is, she means that she accepts her position as a de facto slave and thus
assents to it. Electra will demolish this position, but not until much
later. Chrysothemis' remark about Electra and justice is one of several
times in this play when a character reveals what they are thinking but
not saying openly; in all of those cases those internal thoughts are
governed by Electra. This effect is more visible here than elsewhere,
and so it may be well to consider its significance at this point. When
William Arrowsmith used to discuss this play, he would refer to a passage from John Jay Chapman which still strikes me as particularly apt:

> The radicals are really always saying the same thing. They do not
> change: everybody else changes. They are accused of the most incom-
> patible crimes, of egoism and a mania for power, indifference to the
> fate of their own cause, fanaticism, triviality, want of humor, buffoonery
> and irreverence. [!] But they sound a certain note. Hence the great
> practical power of consistent radicals. To all appearance nobody follows
> them, yet every one believes them. They hold a tuning fork and sound
> A, and everybody knows it really is A, though the time-honored pitch
> is G flat. The community cannot get that A out of its head. Nothing
> can prevent an upward tendency in the popular tone so long as the
> real A is kept sounding. Every now and then the whole town strikes it
> for a week, and all the bells ring, and then all sinks to suppressed
> discord and denial.[16]

When Electra replies to Chrysothemis, she tries to defend herself in
terms of expediency:

. . . what do I stand to gain if I cease my
lament?
Do I not live? Badly, I know, but I live.
What is more,
I am a violation to them.   (478–81)

15. Sophocles, *Philoctetes*, trans. by David Grene, in *Sophocles II*, University of Chicago Press,
1957, lines 1048–52.
16. "A sampling of letters and obiter dicta," edited by William Arrowsmith, *Arion*, third series, 2.2
and 3, 1992/3, p. 64. The passage is from *Practical Agitation*.

"Gain" (*kerdos*) is a word often found in expediency argument—it has the connotation of profit or the bottom line. Perhaps we should note that in the Greek text (l. 354) she says "but I live *sufficiently for me.*" Chrysothemis will later point out that some forms of living are worse than death, and Electra here seems to admit that some level of physical comfort must be present before one can practice virtue. Electra is not simply an embodiment of the justice argument, just as Chrysothemis is not purely the expediency argument. Each is trying to accommodate the opposite view as well as her own.

There is no room for compromise between the justice argument and the expediency argument in this case, and it would be reasonable for this scene to end in mutual rejection, as happens in the parallel scene between Antigone and Ismene, but suddenly Chrysothemis remembers why she has left the palace and she tells about Clytemnestra's dream.

That Clytemnestra had a dream is traditional, but Sophocles has changed its content. In Aeschylus she dreamed that she gave birth to a snake, put it to her breast, and it drew out blood mixed with milk. Here, Agamemnon returns to the light, sticks his scepter into the earth beside the hearth, and the scepter puts forth a branch that overshadows all of Mycenae. Aeschylus' version of the dream emphasized the violation of nature implicated in matricide; Sophocles' emphasizes the return of natural process when the heir returns. In Sophocles' play, it is Electra, not Orestes, who drinks Clytemnestra's blood. We are meant, of course, to recall that in the *Iliad* Achilles said that this very scepter would never bloom again. Here we see how it could bloom again, by the installation of the true heir in the palace.

When Electra asks Chrysothemis to tell of the dream, she makes a remark that hints very broadly at the fact that this is a play of intrigue:

Little words can mean
death or life to someone.   (566–67)

Sophocles' *Electra* is, among other things, a thriller—we enjoy the helplessness of the good characters and their desperate hopes, not to mention the haughty speech of the bad persons, because we are absolutely sure of the outcome.

The immediate effect of the dream is that Electra can now make another appeal to Chrysothemis. Her tone shifts from hostility to pleading. She asks Chrysothemis to throw away the offerings, which she will agree to do, precisely because Clytemnestra will never know. Instead, Electra says, she should take locks of her own hair and Electra's, and

> this belt of mine
> though it's nothing elaborate.   (618–19)

These are "meagre gifts (615)"—literally "little [*smikra*, 615] gifts"—just
as Chrysothemis' words were "little" (*smikroi*) at 566. But they will be
enough. There is a hint here of the justice versus expediency argument.
Electra has nothing but the right, but that nothing is enough. After the
wonderful student performance at the University of Kansas in 1978,[17] I
was offered my choice of props. As I write these words, the belt of
Electra hangs behind me from the ceiling of my office, entangled in
the crown of Aegisthus.

The scene ends on a note of hope and of friendship, far different
from the way it began. The next time Chrysothemis enters, the reverse
will occur. In a play that is filled with emotion, nothing to me is more
affecting than the shifting moods in these two sisters, who are "of one
nature."

When Chrysothemis leaves, the chorus sing their second song. First,
they respond to the dream:

> Unless I am utterly wrong in my reading of
>   omens
> unless I am out of my mind
> Justice is coming
> with clear signs before her
> and righteousness in her hands.   (648–52)

They are not wrong, of course—we know that Orestes is momentarily
to appear. The dream is a clear sign of the approach of Justice. As often
in the comments of this chorus, there seems to be a hint of the traditional story. The theme of Justice is prominent in Aeschylus' version. These lines are also what we would expect in a play of action.
They inform us that Apollo's plan is working out; Orestes will soon
appear.

In their final stanza, the mood and subject suddenly shift: "O
horserace of Pelops, . . ." (678). Pelops, the person who founded the
royal family at Argos, whose members include Orestes, Electra, and
Aegisthus, bribed Myrtilus, the charioteer of the king Oinomaus, to rig
the king's chariot so that Pelops might win the race and so take the
daughter of Oinomaus as his bride. After the race, in which Oinomaus

17. See note 6.

was killed, Pelops also killed Myrtilus. No wonder Orestes thought of the story that he had been killed in a chariot crash. But the chorus refer to this old story because they think they have found a principle at work in this family:

> never
> since that time
> has this house
> got itself clear of
> rawblood
> butchery. (686–91)

They used the same word at the beginning of the song: the axe was used "to butcher the meat." It is a good word to end on. The butcher herself now enters.

Clytemnestra has a servant with her who carries offerings to be sacrificed. Thus we can see that she is of higher rank than Chrysothemis, who carried her offerings in her own hands. But in its general structure this scene resembles the preceding one: a woman enters with offerings, is diverted when she sees Electra and is drawn into an argument, after which she reveals the purpose of the offerings. Then the sacrifice is performed, offstage or on, but it has been altered by Electra. This parallel in the action suggests that Electra is dominating Clytemnestra's thoughts, just as she is those of Chrysothemis.

Clytemnestra does not make any pretense of politeness when she begins:

> Prowling the streets again, are you?
> Of course, with Aegisthus away. (692–93)

Her first point, that Electra "embarrass[es] us," 695, has already been raised by Electra, who has admitted from the start that her behavior is shameful. But she quickly changes tack: "It was Justice who took him, not I alone" (705). When the Greek fleet was about to sail for Troy, it was becalmed at the Greek port of Aulis, and only the sacrifice of Agamemnon's daughter Iphigenia would gain favoring winds for the Greek fleet. She also claimed that she murdered Agamemnon to avenge Iphigenia in Aeschylus' *Agamemnon*. Clytemnestra has a strong case—indeed, its merits are still being discussed. Furthermore, Sophocles puts her case strongly, at one point even letting her sound like one of his heroines:

> Did he have some share
> in the pain of her birth? No—I did it myself!
>
> (711–12)

To an audience member who knows his Aeschylus and who routinely thinks in terms of justice versus expediency, it seems that Clytemnestra has challenged Electra on her own ground.

Electra attempts to refute Clytemnestra's justice argument by offering another version of the events at Aulis, in which Agamemnon had no choice but to sacrifice his daughter. This is not a particularly effective counter to Clytemnestra's argument, whose strongest point is that Agamemnon has violated Clytemnestra's rights as a mother. Even worse is the principle she cites at the end of her justice argument:

> By what law?
> Watch out: this particular law
> could recoil upon your own head.
> If we made it a rule
> to answer killing with killing,
> you would die first,
> in all justice.   (777–83)

If this is true of Clytemnestra, it is also true of Orestes and Electra. But I do not think that we should follow the extreme version of the dark reading and assume that this shows that Electra is profoundly mistaken. For one thing, in the mythical time line, so to speak, the world of some higher form of justice than an eye for an eye is still to come. Indeed, Orestes is going to be the catalyst for its appearance.

More important, we must keep the context of this defective justice argument in mind. In the overall structure of this speech, it is not presented as the main argument. Electra began on quite a different note:

> All right then. Yes.
> You killed my father, you admit.
> What admission could bring more shame?
> Never mind if it was legal or not—did you
>   care?   (749–52)

Carson's translation catches the disdain of Electra for the legal issues involved here. She is mainly interested in reverence (*eusebeia*). Once she has ended her justice argument, Electra returns to this main theme of shame (emphasis added to line 791):

Tell me:
why do you live this way?
Your life is filth [*aischista*, (most shameful)]
You share your bed with a bloodstained man:
once he obliged you by killing my father,
now you put him to use making children.
Once you had *decent* children from a *decent*
father
    [*eusebeis . . . eusebon* (reverent . . .
    reverent)],
now you've thrown them out.   (785–92)

She ends her speech with an explosive rejoinder to Clytemnestra's original charge that she was embarrassing her friends:

for if this is my nature
we know how I come by it, don't we?
    (817–18)

The chorus draw attention to the passions of this speech:

Look. Anger is breathing out of her.
Yet she seems not to care
about right and wrong.   (819–21)

Although Anne Carson's stage directions state here that these lines refer to Clytemnestra's apparently visible anger at Electra's speech, I assume that they refer to Electra herself. Scholars are divided, and the reader must decide. However, if the lines refer to Electra, as I believe, their remarks here support those who feel that Electra has simply lost control of her emotions. However, her points are valid and one does not talk about good and bad conduct in neutral terms. Clytemnestra's marriage to Aegisthus and her neglect of her children by Agamemnon are indefensible. Her subsequent behavior in this scene shows that she cannot answer these charges. One is left then with the impression that Electra has won this encounter where *reverence* is the issue, but that she has failed with respect to *justice*.

Clytemnestra herself breaks off the discussion which she had initiated:

By Artemis I swear, you will pay for this
when Aegisthus comes home.   (845–46)

Electra points out that she has turned from argument to threat. Clytemnestra makes no response, but instead asks Electra to be silent so she can make her sacrifice.

In the prayer which follows, Clytemnestra cannot speak freely because Electra is watching her. She tells Apollo that she must make a "guarded" (861) prayer. She cannot ask that Orestes not return, but instead she asks for "everything to go on as it is, / untroubled" (876–77). This remark's falsity is proved by the very conditions of this speech. Her behavior here also undercuts her earlier claim that "I feel no remorse" (737). She will admit to her true inner feelings once she thinks Orestes is dead.

She ends her speech in a conventional way, but what happens next gives it an unintended meaning:

> CLYTEMNESTRA It goes without saying,
> the children of Zeus see all things.
> Amen.

> OLD MAN Ladies, can you tell me for certain
> if this is the house of Aegisthus the king?
>
> (890–94)

Apollo has heard her prayer, and he responds. The Old Man will seem to bring her the answer to her prayers. We expect this kind of misdirection from Apollo, the great riddler, of whom the early philosopher Heraclitus said, "The god at Delphi does not say; he does not conceal; he gives a sign."

When the Old Man enters, a new stage in the sufferings of Electra begins. This process begins with a sudden jolt:

> OLD MAN Orestes is dead. That is the sum of it.

> ELECTRA OI 'GO TALAINA
> My death begins now.

> CLYTEMNESTRA What are you saying, what are you saying?
> Don't bother with her. (907–11)

This short passage indicates to us the response that the two women will display through gesture during the Old Man's long and exciting speech.

Once the speech has ended, Clytemnestra responds:

> To give birth is terrible, incomprehensible.
> No matter how you suffer,
> you cannot hate a child you've born.
>
> (1042–44)

How do we take what she says here? There is no reason to doubt her sincerity. It is possible to conclude that some compromise between her and her children is possible and that the vengeance is wrong.[18] However, she will admit that she thinks Orestes' death is a good thing just a few moments later. Seen in the full context of the scene, it would appear that Sophocles has simply given his Clytemnestra a human touch.[19]

The Old Man suggests that he should not have come, and she immediately admits that she feels relief. Because of Orestes' constant threats, "Time stood like a deathmaster over me . . . / Now I am free" (1056–58). In her elation, she reveals thoughts she has denied until now:

> And to tell you the truth,
> she did more damage.
> She lived in my house
> and drank
> my lifeblood neat!
>
> (1061–65)

Although she claimed that she felt no remorse when she first entered the stage (737), here she admits that she has been enervated and depressed. Her reference to Electra's drinking her blood shows that in her own mind Electra is something like a Fury.[20] Electra accuses Clytemnestra of *hybris* ("Orestes . . . your own mother insults you" 1071, 1073), and gets her to express her pleasure at Orestes' death more openly:

> Well you're no fine sight.
> But he looks as fine as can be.
>
> (1075–76)

Fine maternal feeling here!

At the end of this scene, Clytemnestra is still very much aware of Electra:

---

18. "And in this scene he subtly transfers our sympathy to her" (Kells, 8).

19. This remark was made about her by Professor Jack Wright in his critique of the production I observed.

20. R. P. Winnington-Ingram (n.12 above), p. 233: "For all her bravado, she lived in fear."

> Stranger, you deserve a reward
> if you really have put a stop on her traveling
>   tongue. (1082–83)

And her exit line is also concerned with her:

> Just leave her out here
> to go on with her evil litany. (1088–89)

An audience steeped in this story might see here that Electra performs a function like that of a Fury, as a "distracter" (*parakopa*, [*Eumenides*, 339]). In the similar scene in Aeschylus' *Libation Bearers*, Clytemnestra sends the messenger (in this version, Orestes himself) to the men's quarters and later sends a message for Aegisthus to come with his bodyguard. In this play, Clytemnestra sends no such message, and when Orestes arrives he is welcomed into the main hall where he stands beside Clytemnestra as she prepares the urn for burial. One reason that she does not show more caution is the distraction caused by Electra.

Electra is alone on stage with the chorus, and she speaks of the effect on her of Orestes' death:

> You have torn away the part of my mind
> where hope was—
> my one hope in you (1096–98)

She had said at the beginning of the play that Orestes was her only hope. Now that support is gone, and "Life is no desire of mine anymore" (1117). She says that she will "lie / unloved" before the door to the palace (1111–12), and I assume she sings the following dialogue from a lying position, her physical position mirroring her mental depression.

The chorus immediately turn to the gods, "Where are you lightnings of Zeus!" (1119). Electra resists; she does not want to turn to false hopes. The chorus think of a parallel (they often do)—Amphiaraus, one of the Seven Against Thebes. Electra counters that he is a bad choice because his son avenged him by killing his mother. Electra remains focused on what she can do, on deeds with her own hands, like other Sophoclean heroes, and so she ends the *kommos*:

> Laid out
> somewhere
> not by my hands.
> Not with my tears. (1162–65)

The mood abruptly shifts when Chrysothemis enters:

> I am so happy, I ran here to tell you—
> decorum aside! (1166–67)

This should mark the beginning of the discovery and of the change of Electra's fortunes. Chrysothemis is absolutely certain that Orestes has returned: "I saw the evidence with my own eyes" (1181); yet she is easily persuaded by Electra that she is wrong ("What a fool I am . . ." 1236). Once again, Electra dominates the action.

Electra suddenly shifts to a new topic:

> . . . But listen to me.
> You could ease our sorrow. (1240–1)

Chrysothemis responds to this with her characteristic common sense: "How? Raise the dead?"(1242) Chrysothemis agrees to display some "nerve," but with a significant condition: "If it *benefits* us, I will not refuse" (1246) (emphasis added). This is the language of expediency, and we know that this scene is headed into the same impasse with which their first scene began.

We expect talk here of loyalty, honor, and justice from Electra, and we will get it. But first she attacks Chrysothemis' expediency position with an unexpected vigor and clarity:

> Let's be blunt, girl, what hope is left?
> Your losses are mounting,
> the property gone and
> marriage
> seems a fading dream at your age—
> or do you still console yourself with thoughts
>   of a husband?
> Forget it. Aegisthus is not so naive
> as to see children born from you or from me—
> unambiguous grief for himself. (1263–72)

Electra has destroyed Chrysothemis' position in her own terms. She has lost the property, and can never have children. In terms of benefit, little is left to her.

Chrysothemis' reply is equally strong. Her first argument, that they will fail if they try to kill Aegisthus, will only convince those so disposed. But failure is not the only prospect here, and Chrysothemis refers to two more:

> Death itself is not the worst thing.
> Worse is to live
> when you want to die.
> So I beg you,
> before you destroy us
> and wipe out the family altogether,
> control your temper. (1323–29)

Electra has already admitted the validity of this first point in their first scene when she said she lived "sufficiently for me" (my translation of line 354 in the Greek, line 479 in this translation). In Athens, slaves who were to give evidence in court were routinely broken on the rack. There are no illusions in such a place about the ability of human nature to endure anything. The second point is that one cannot pursue honor to the extent that it threatens the city or the family. This, too, an Athenian would recognize as valid. Chrysothemis and Electra are both advancing their arguments in very strong form, and so it is clear that there is no room here for compromise.

Electra suddenly shifts; instead of urging Chrysothemis to act, or castigating her, she turns to what she is suffering at Chrysothemis' hands:

> ELECTRA At least realize you are driving me into
> dishonor.

> CHRYSOTHEMIS Dishonor? No: foresight. (1362–63)

The word "dishonor" is important to Electra; Electra's life is devoted to honoring the dead (482). Chrysothemis' desertion of her is one in a series of dishonorings.

When Chrysothemis leaves, Electra appears to have lost all of her allies among the living. In this desperate situation, something unusual happens, so far as Sophoclean choruses are concerned. They depart from their usual caution and good sense, and they praise Electra precisely because she is powerless, "betrayed, / alone" (1422–23). They praise her because she does *not* have forethought:

> Nor
> does she think

> to fear dying,
> no! (1430–33)

They end their song with an emphatic use of a word that means a great deal to Electra:

> you are the one who kept faith
> with the living laws,
> kept faith
> in the clear reverence
> of Zeus. (1462–66)

The word "reverence," which has been so important one for Electra, is the entrance cue for Orestes. It is the moment of reversal, surely. But as soon as he enters, we realize that he will appear to be something quite different to Electra than the end of her troubles:

> ORESTES We have his remains in a small jar here—
> for he's dead, as you see. (1484–45)

There could be no greater difference between what Electra sees and what she thinks she sees. Orestes, carrying out divine commands, will now push Electra even further into despair.

Orestes gives the urn to Electra, and she delivers a speech that was famous in antiquity and that remains emotionally powerful today. Although she occasionally refers to her specific situation, on the whole this is an extensive and accurate description of the feelings one has at the death of a loved person. The chorus think her grief is excessive ("be reasonable," 1571), but we do not share in that feeling because we know that everything will soon be all right.

Another reason for the power of this speech is the purity of spirit that Electra reveals. Reverence has been her theme word, and this speech is largely about reverence as it is acted out by a noble daughter and sister. She begins by addressing the urn itself, lamenting that her hopes have been dashed because Orestes now is "nothing" (1510), and then recalls how she saved him with her own hands (1513). She moves quickly to the next act with her hands that "reverence" would have required of her:

> And I would have waited
> and washed you ["with my loving hands," the
> Greek adds here]

and lifted you
up from the fire. . . .   (1522–25)

She addresses her wasted nurture of Orestes ("years of my love," 1532; the Greek here refers to "a sweet labor").

Now she considers the loss of Orestes from another perspective. His death meant also the disappearance of Agamemnon and the death of Electra. From Orestes the person she nursed she turns to Orestes who had promised vengeance on her mother. This is her first overt reference to Clytemnestra's death, but those who see this as sign of Electra's bloody mindedness take the comment out of context. For one thing, she says Orestes has been saying that he would take vengeance on Clytemnestra, and although Electra says here that Orestes' return would be "secret" (1549), Clytemnestra knew what he had been threatening to do (1054). For another, Electra herself is stressing loss, not the revenge that will never be. The thought begins "One day three people vanished" (1542), and so her reference to her enemies and to her mother are illustrations of the nothingness that she now sees all around her.

She considers Orestes' remains again, his "ashes" (1554), and says he is a "shadow" (an image of human insignificance Sophocles has used before).[21] By dying he has destroyed her, and she wishes to join him in the urn:

Oh my love
take me there.
Let me dwell where you are.
I am already nothing.
I am already burning.
Oh my love, I was once part of you —
take me too!
Only void is between us.
And I see that the dead feel no pain.

(1562–70)

When Electra says "take me there," she means "take me into the urn with you," as the Greek text makes clear. There is an echo here of the greatest friendship in Greek literature; the ghost of Achilles' best friend, Patroclus, asked Achilles to have his ashes placed in the same urn as his own (*Iliad*, Book 23, lines 91–92).

21. Odysseus says that all human beings are "shadows of smoke," *Aias*, 126.

The reference to herself as "nothing" (1565) echoes what other Sophoclean heroes say about themselves, or have others say about them, at similar moments of ultimate evil fortune.[22] Although they are "nobodies," because of their extravagant failures, they are powerful in a fashion that is visible on the stage. For instance, in *Ajax*, when Ajax's brother Teucer defends Ajax's right to burial, even though he had committed treason against the army, Agamemnon says that Teucer (a bastard) is "a nobody" who is standing up for a "nobody" (i.e., a dead man, 1231), just a few lines before Odysseus, Ajax's political enemy, arrives to defend him.

In this case, the person who will make Electra into the opposite of a "nothing" is standing beside her. Once again, a character in this play speaks lines that have a meaning in themselves, but they are given additional meaning because other characters are silently responding to those lines. It is not possible to say how much business Sophocles assigned to Orestes while this speech is going on. His mere presence on stage tells us that her suffering will soon end. But he also must be indicating the sympathy he will express soon after the speech ends.

The chorus respond with traditional consolation for one who is grieving a death, but at this point there is a sudden shift. It is not Electra who responds to them, but the other character, Orestes:

> What should I say? This is
> impossible! I cannot hold my tongue much
> longer.   (1576–77)

The moment we have been waiting for since the first lines of the play has arrived, and yet there is one more excruciating delay. Orestes has one request that to him seems trivial enough, but it leads to another emotional outburst:

> ORESTES Give back the urn, then, and you will hear
> everything.
>
> ELECTRA No! Don't take this from me, for Gods' sake,
> whoever you are.
>
> ORESTES Come now, do as I say. It is the right thing.

22. The other passages are *Oedipus Tyrannus*, 1188; *Oedipus at Colonus* 393; *Trachiniae*, 1107; *Philoctetes* 1030. Only in the *Oedipus Tyrannus* is this paradoxical power not immediately visible. But even in that play the main character shows a strength that belies Creon's final line, in which he says that Oedipus' power has not followed him to the end (1523).

> ELECTRA No! In all reverence no please—don't take this
>   away.
>   It is all that I love.   (1610–15)

Again, Sophocles draws our attention to the stripping away from Electra
of all that she cares for. And then he shows her losing yet one thing
more.

> ELECTRA Wrong to mourn my own dead brother?

> ORESTES Wrong for you to say that word.

> ELECTRA How did I lose the right to call him brother?
>   (1622–24)

A more literal rendering of that last line would be "Am I so dishonored
by the dead?" This word, "dishonored" (*atimos*), means a lot to Electra.
When she defended herself to Chrysothemis the first time, she used
the word "honor":

> I am a violation to them.
> And so, honor [*timas prosaptein*] the dead—
> if any grace exists down there.   (481–83)

That the dead should not reciprocate the honor she has spent her life
granting them is an annihilating thought.

This reference to being "dishonored" is the point of Electra's most
complete degradation. In the very next line Orestes assures her that
she has her honor: "Your rights you have" (1625). In my experience,
this is the most emotional passage in this drama. We have watched this
stripping of Electra even longer than Orestes has. She sums that stripping up in one word, "dishonored." There has been no validation of
her action, except by the chorus. With Orestes' remark, her isolation
has ended. We assent to his remark, and we feel relief that at last
Electra knows the secret we have known since the beginning.

I would like to pause at this moment, just before Orestes announces
that honor is hers by right, to ask why Sophocles should bring Electra
to this point, stripped of everything she depends on. There is a discussion of this problem in Tom Gould's last book, which has been of help

to me.[23] Professor Gould observed that the passions aroused by literature were at the heart of the discussion of tragedy by Plato and Aristotle,
although the passions are largely overlooked in modern criticism.[24]
Plato would ban the sufferings (*pathe*) of Niobe, of the children of
Pelops, and of Troy.[25] Aristotle admits in *Poetics* that suffering is necessary to the tragic, but he argues that our response to this suffering
has a beneficial purpose, whatever "*katharsis*" may mean.

Gould claims that Sophocles "brought the thrilling *pathe* of hero
religion right into the theater and evidently felt that no explanation or
apology was needed." That is, Sophoclean tragedy enables us to respond to the suffering and death that are part of human existence. In
this play, those heroic sufferings occur in a special context: we know
that Electra's sufferings are already over. And yet, this is one of the
most tearful of all Greek dramas.[26] Perhaps we can only face hopeless-
ness and death as fully as we do here when we are certain that everything will turn out all right.

But there is another explanation that I would like to suggest here.
The stripping away of every support from Electra is reminiscent of a
case posed by Glaukon in the *Republic* of Plato. Glaukon asks Socrates
to compare two men, and to say who is the happier. The first man is
completely unjust, but he has the reputation of being just and is suc-
cessful in every way. Here is the second man, in Cornford's translation:

> Now set beside this paragon the just man in his simplicity and noble-
> ness, one who, in Aeschylus' words, 'would be, not seem, the best.'
> There must, indeed, be no such seeming; for if his character were
> apparent, his reputation would bring him honours and rewards, and
> then we should not know whether it was for their sake that he was just
> or for justice's sake alone. He must be stripped of everything but justice,
> and denied every advantage the other enjoyed. Doing no wrong, he
> must have the worst reputation for wrong-doing, to test whether his
> virtue is proof against all that comes of having a bad name; and under

23. Thomas Gould, *The Ancient Quarrel Between Poetry and Philosophy*, Princeton University
Press, 1991.
24. One classical scholar who did treat the passions in drama was Friedrich Nietzsche, whose
book *The Birth of Tragedy* was first published in German in 1872. Another was Karl Reinhardt,
whose *Sophokles*, first published in 1933, was translated by Hazel Harvey and David Harvey from
the German in 1979 (Oxford: Basil Blackwell). More recently, W. B. Stanford, *Greek Tragedy and
the Emotions: An Introductory Study*, London and Boston: Routledge and Kegan Paul, 1983, notes
there is "no comprehensive book on the subject" (p. 1). There are some remarks in Oliver Taplin,
Greek Tragedy in Action, Berkeley and Los Angeles: University of California Press, 1978; in particular, see chapter 10, "Emotion and Meaning in the Theatre."
25. *Republic* 2.380a 5–7.
26. There is a wonderful account by Fiona Shaw of the emotional impact of this play in Francis
M. Dunn, editor, *Sophocles' "Electra" in Performance*, Stuttgart: M&P, 1996.

> this lifelong imputation of wickedness, let him hold on his course of
> justice unwavering to the point of death. And so, when the two men
> have carried their justice and injustice to the last extreme, we may
> judge which is the happier. (361b5–d3)[27]

Electra fits this situation from the beginning: she is a "just [woman]
in (her) simplicity and nobleness," but she has "the worst reputation
for wrong-doing." Like the man Glaukon imagines, Electra lacks both
"rewards" and "honors" (*timai*).

This play poses the question of Glaukon, and it offers an answer.
This answer is largely found in the play's action, in those many cases
where it is implied that the other characters are under the authority of
Electra, accepting that what she says is true and just. Thus, Orestes
says something that we already know when he replies to Electra, "Your
rights you have" (1625). The exact phrasing of this line is significant;
here is a closer version: "You are dishonored [*atimos*] by no one—that
is not what is appropriate for you" (1215 in the Greek). This line thus
refers to the phenomenon Arrowsmith had noted and that he thought
John Jay Chapman had best expressed. That is, not only is it true that
the dead honor Electra; everyone honors Electra. Chrysothemis' admission that Electra has justice on her side is honor. Clytemnestra's
anguished mental state is honor as well. Everyone is taking their signal
from Electra. Like Chapman's radical who sounds the note "A," Electra
sounds "the just," and the just, in this play, is conversely what Electra
sounds. This is why Clytemnestra's very-good-justice argument col-
lapses and vanishes. Chrysothemis even assumes that whatever Electra
says is true and doubts the evidence of her own eyes.

Electra has also been "happy" throughout this play. Electra herself
explains how this could be so to Chrysothemis: she has an adequate
life and she harms her enemies and honors her friends (479–82). On
most realistic assessments this statement describes a happy life. But
there is more to the answer than this: The play shows us Electra living
on a different level of intensity from anyone else.

Orestes gives us a hint of this intensity early in this discovery scene,
in which he uses the word "brilliant" ("famous" [*kleinon*] 1579) to describe her: "Is this the brilliant Electra?" This word usually refers to a
heroic reputation The usual explanation is that Electra is famous because of who her father was (as Orestes is "famous"),[28] but it seems to

---

27. *The Republic of Plato*, translated with introduction and notes by Francis MacDonald Cornford,
New York: Oxford University Press, 1945.

28. *Sophocles . . . Part VI. The Electra*, edited by Sir Richard C. Jebb, Cambridge: At the University
Press, 1907, note on line 1177.

me that we have been aware that she is indeed "famous" since the beginning of the play, when Orestes wanted to wait and see her.

After Orestes has revealed himself and they have expressed their joy at being reunited, they shift to song and express the same emotions. Electra is lyric in mood and in meter; Orestes keeps urging her to control herself in prosaic iambic. Electra's opening lines are of considerable interest:

> IO GONAI.
> You exist!
> You came back,
> you found me—   (1650–53)

One scholar translates the Greek text translated here as "You exist" literally as "Ah! birth—birth of a person to me most beloved . . ."[29] This is not a normal form of address, but Orestes is the legitimate offspring (another meaning of *gone*), and it seems only apt that Electra, whose very name means the suppression of offspring,[30] should use it. When Electra cries out that word she announces her release from that perverted marriage that she has been forced to witness and from the virginity forced on her by that polluted coupling. The manifest result of the deeds of Aegisthus and Clytemnestra has been the perversion of marriage and birth. Clytemnestra's legitimate children cannot inherit, and they cannot marry.

In the midst of this outpouring of love, Electra, for a chilling moment, remembers the horror of her past life:

> ELECTRA Do not turn your face from me.
>   Don't take yourself away.

> ORESTES Of course not. No one else will take me
>   either.

> ELECTRA Do you mean that?

> ORESTES Yes I do.   (1701–5)

She reminds us, for a moment, of what she has had to see and what she has been forced not to see, all these years.

---

29. Kells, note on 1232 ff.
30. See the notes on 663–69 and 1266–67.

The singing ends, and Orestes immediately speaks as the cool planner: "We've no time for all that" (1722). Electra agrees to help her brother and to deceive her mother in order to serve "the *daimon* who is now at hand," their momentary good luck—"the god who stands beside us now," as Carson puts it (1740). This is a remarkable thing for a person to say who has been so closely identified with justice. Her own explanation is that she is so happy to see Orestes again that she can deny him in nothing. Perhaps we can forgive her this inconsistency because it is her heart that leads her to it. But one has come to expect so much of this woman. She ends this speech with a reminiscence of herself before her luck changed, Electra alone, desperate, and heroic:

> Alone,
> I would have done one of two things:
> deliver myself or else die.　　　　　(1760–62)

The Old Man enters and urges them to hurry up. Orestes asks him how his mother has taken the news of his death. Another awkward moment; the Old Man does not tell all he knows:

> ORESTES Are they happy at this?

> OLD MAN I'll tell you that later. For now,
> 　　　　the whole plan is unfolding beautifully.
> 　　　　Even the ugly parts.　　　　　(1786–89)

What the Old Man means is not entirely clear. Some have suggested that he means that Clytemnestra's motherly feelings have distracted her and caused her to be taken in by the trick even more easily. Kells thinks that is what he means, and he concludes that Clytemnestra is not the evil woman Orestes and Electra take her to be.[31] However, there is plenty of evidence in this scene of her pleasure at Orestes' death and Electra's defeat. There is another possibility. In Aeschylus' trilogy, that evil gives rise to good is a pervasive theme; for instance, Athena says of the Furies in the *Eumenides*: "I see great profit to these citizens, coming out of those fearful faces" (990–91). The Old Man may well be referring to the broadest outlines of this traditional story.

Electra asks who the Old Man is, and upon learning that he is the very person into whose hands she committed the infant Orestes, she again breaks out in joy:

31. Kells, note on 1344.

> Bless you, father!—Yes, father.
> That is who I see when I look at you now.
> There is no man on earth I have hated and
>   loved like you
> on the one same day.   (1814–17)

It has been suggested that Electra's words here indicate mental instability.[32] That she is excited is undeniable. However, it is not irrational for her to see in the Old Man the reincarnation of her father. As the agent of Justice, the Old Man represents the dead man. For the same reason, it is reasonable for her to bless his hands and his feet. The chorus has earlier described Vengeance as having many hands and many feet (663–64).

The ending of this scene suggests that Electra has not lost sight of her guiding principles, despite her excitement. After Orestes and Pylades bow to the gods before the house and go in, Electra prays:

> show
> how the gods reward
> unholy action! [*dys-sebeia*, "irreverence"]
>   (1843–45)

The word "reverence" introduced this scene (1465). After the excitement caused by Orestes' appearance, she has regained her focus.

The chorus now sing their third stasimon, which is very brief, as Sophocles' lyrics often are when the climactic action is about to occur. Once again their language recalls the traditional form of this story. Orestes and Pylades are identified with Furies, "the raw and deadly dogs" (1850). The statement that "Hermes . . . guides him" (1857) also has an archaic sound; in Aeschylus' *Eumenides*, Hermes was a silent character who guided Orestes from Delphi to Athens.

The lyrics continue when Electra returns to the stage. Clytemnestra is heard off-stage, appealing to Orestes. Electra enjoys this awful event. These are grim lines:

> CLYTEMNESTRA O child my child, pity the mother who bore
>   you!
>
> ELECTRA Yet you had little enough pity for him
>   and none for his father!   (1875–77)

32. Kells, p. 11.

Harsh words but true. But Electra does not relent when Clytemnestra cries out:

> CLYTEMNESTRA OMOI
> I am hit!

> ELECTRA Hit her a second time, if you have the
> strength!

> CLYTEMNESTRA OMOI MAL' AUTHIS.
> Again!

> ELECTRA If only Aegisthus could share this!
>   (1882–87)

There is no question that her words are harsh. But it is not clear what Electra means when she says "if you have the strength." Sophocles was famous for drawing a character in a single line and this time he has made only two words do the work of many: "does not *ei stheneis* ["if you have the strength"] imply something more than is to be expressed by loud and complicated lyrical lamentations about her feelings at that dreadful moment?"[33] This is true, of course, but there is also some significance in the fact that she spoke of those turbulent inner feelings. Even here, she is not so ignorant of the inner forces driving her as Aeschylus' Clytemnestra or Euripides' Electra. But she does not weaken; she looks forward to dealing with Aegisthus (1887).

When Orestes enters, stained with blood, he and Electra have a short but significant exchange. This is a moment of great danger—one where one could commit a regrettable excess, or reveal mental instability. In their brief dialogue, both are markedly restrained:

> ELECTRA Orestes, how does it go?

> ORESTES Good, so far—at least so far as Apollo's oracle
> was good.   (1897–99)

In the dark reading, this line can be taken to mean that Apollo's oracle was not valid, but Orestes himself means that it is for Apollo to say whether this was a good deed. In the Aeschylean version, he actually

---

33. J. T. Sheppard, "The Tragedy of Electra, According to Sophocles," [n. 4, above] p. 88.

goes to Delphi after the murder and proceeds according to Apollo's instructions. There is also an echo here of the *Odyssey*. When the old nurse sees that the suitors are dead and is about to shout out in triumph, Odysseus restrains her by insisting that he was acting in accord with the gods:

> No cries of triumph now.
> It's unholy to glory over the bodies of the
>   dead.
> These men the doom of the gods has brought
>   low,
> and their own indecent acts.[34]

Electra is not satisfied with this answer. She must know exactly what happened:

> ELECTRA Is the creature dead?
>
> ORESTES Your good mother will not insult you any-
>   more.   (1900–1901)

The Greek word translated here as "creature" means nothing more than "wretch," the person who has suffered. If anything, it indicates some slight compassion.

In Orestes' response, the word here translated "insult" literally means "dishonor" (*atimesei*), and echoes his line that was discussed earlier, "You are dishonored [*atimos*] by no one—that is not what is appropriate for you." In both cases, Orestes reveals that relieving Electra of her dishonor is constantly on his mind and has almost the same status as the oracle of Apollo.

After this dialogue ends, the chorus see that Aegisthus is coming. They are in the spirit of things now: "You have won the first round. Now for the second" (1908). They are no more troubled by deceit now than Electra seems to be: "Why not drop a few friendly words in his ear" (1913).

Aegisthus speaks in the manner of a tyrant from the beginning. He makes no formal address but begins with a question, "Does anyone know . . ." (1916). His address to Electra is even more insulting:

---

34. Homer, *Odyssey*, translated by Robert Fagles, N.Y.: Penguin Books, 1996, Book 22, lines 436–39 (lines 411–13 in the Greek text).

> You!
> yes you!—you've never been shy
> to speak your mind. (1919–21)

He is completely lacking in sympathy—he asks her about the news because Orestes was a concern to her. He speaks as a tyrant when he orders the gates opened:

> take my bit on your tongue
> or learn the hard way. (1940–42)

Creon also spoke of his rule as a "bit" when he was at his harshest (*Antigone*, 477). Electra plays along: "As for me, I am playing my part to the end" (1942). It appears that she is opening the gates herself—no matter what Aegisthus says, on this stage Electra is in control. She obeys him with a sarcastic acceptance of expedience: "I've learned to side with the winners" (1943). Electra toys with Aegisthus. Some have found this baiting distasteful. There is a danger of excess, and she is close to the limit.

Aegisthus removes the cover from the body, expecting to find Orestes, and finds Clytemnestra instead. This is one of the most exciting moments in Greek tragedy. However, before Aegisthus raises the cover, Sophocles adds a subtle touch to his character. Up until this point, Aegisthus has been presented purely as a villain, but after he has said that the gods have caused Orestes' death, Sophocles has him restrain himself: "if that remark offends, / I unsay it" (1946–47). By making this qualification, Aegisthus shows just enough human decency to make him a believable human being.

Aegisthus raises the sheet, realizes that he has been trapped, and asks (in the language of Aeschylus' version of the story) "whose is the net?" (a closer translation than "*who set the trap?*" 1960) Orestes answers with another Aeschylean phrase:

> Don't you realize yet
> that you're talking to dead men alive?
> (1961–62)

Just as when a messenger in the Aeschylean *Libation Bearers* says that "the dead are killing the living" (886), the word "the dead" refers to Orestes, but there is also the hint that Agamemnon himself is acting with Orestes.

To this point, the revenge has proceeded without major hindrance.

Electra's savage remarks about hitting her mother a second time were unsettling, but Orestes' comments that Apollo sanctioned the murder and that Clytemnestra had maltreated Electra were restrained and persuasive. Indeed, we expect the actual butchering of the villains to be unproblematic since the play to this point has given us plenty of reasons to assent to it.

This is not the case. A number of troubling things occur between lines 1968 and 2003. Electra refuses to let Aegisthus speak (1953–63), invoking a principle that calls her dedication to justice into question and displays a brutality that makes us doubt her human decency. With his final words, Orestes recommends the death penalty for every transgression of law (2001–3), and this indicates a fundamental misunderstanding of justice and an insane trust in violence.

I have stated these difficulties in their strongest form because so much is at stake here. I personally believe in the noble Electra— I carry her with me as an "imagined other." She is part of my own moral dialogue. Further, after struggling with these problematic lines, I am convinced that Sophocles intended us to struggle with them.

Aegisthus, accepting that he has lost, asks permission to speak. At this moment Electra breaks in:

> No!
> Don't let him speak—
> by the gods! Brother—no speechmaking now!
> When a human being is so steeped in evil as
>   this one
> what is gained by delaying his death?
>
> (1968–72)

It is not clear exactly what the phrase translated "steeped in evils" means,[35] but whatever that phrase means, the remark that there is no benefit in letting the accused make speeches reveals an astounding ignorance of the nature of justice. In Aeschylus' *Oresteia*, the next phase of this story, when Orestes defends himself at the trial in Athens, is largely concerned with the importance of persuasion. I do not think we can defend this statement. Since her justice argument to Clytem-

---

35. This phrase could mean either "considering all the evils in which all of us are tangled" (referring to the whole messy history of the family) or "considering all the evils he has done" (referring to his adultery and murder). Even if she refers to his adultery, he has the right to speak, even though the death penalty is appropriate and treated as unproblematic in Aeschylus.

nestra earlier was also flawed, I would suggest that she is consistently
wrong about larger abstract issues.

What Electra says next is more troubling:

> Kill him at once.
> Throw his corpse out
> for scavengers to get.   (1973–75)

Electra remains true to her own immediate experience when she says
that she wants the body "unseen by us" (not translated here). It was
the sight of Aegisthus that disgusted her. What she says about disposing
of the body is not so easily excused. Dishonoring a dead body was a
sign of excess in both *Antigone* and *Ajax*. If Electra means to feed
Aegisthus to the dogs, one might argue that she is no longer human.
As so often in these critical passages, we must examine what she says
closely. The issue is not whether Electra expects Aegisthus' body to be
eaten by dogs and birds. She does, and in one version of the story this
was what happened. Rather, it is whether this is something that she
intends to enforce. In the other cases, the ruler announced penalties
against anyone who buried the corpse. In the Greek text, Electra says
it is "likely" (*eikos*, 1488) that he will get a certain kind of "grave-
diggers" (a closer translation than "scavengers"). Nonetheless, it seems
to me unworthy of her even to consider what will happen to his body.
That the dead are dead and that it is insane to punish a body is a
truism in Greek tragedy. On the other hand, Electra's final lines seem
to me to be carefully restrained:

> Nothing less than this
> can cut the knot of evils
> inside me.   (1976–78)

Electra says nothing of the future; rather, she speaks solely of release
from the past. And this she will surely get. Whatever lies ahead for her,
she will not be forced to witness the disgusting behavior of Clytemnestra and Aegisthus.

This short passage forces us to consider the dark reading. The question is not whether Electra is stained by the events of this play. Rather,
it is to what degree she has been stained. Karl Reinhardt takes a balanced position:

> she appears in a world of the wicked and the false as the extreme of
> great-heartedness which enables normal humanity to survive; she is the

woman who loves and hates from the depths of her heart; because of her hate and her love, she suffers, is persecuted, and is even alienated from herself, disfigured, and consumed by her own fires.[36]

I would suggest that this view still gives too much weight to the negative aspects of Electra. Just as Clytemnestra had a touch of maternal feeling and Aegisthus a touch of decency, so Electra has a touch of the madness produced by bloodshed. She is not one of the raging madwomen of the stage, as Kells describes her. Rather, she is a person we admire and care for. We are pained to see her take on any taint. Thus we cannot completely dismiss the dark reading. Kells goes too far when he sees her becoming mad, but Sheppard's more subtle Electra is the one I have delineated here.

After Electra makes her intervention, Orestes and Aegisthus each seek to control the situation. Orestes, as has been noted, wants to introduce a symmetry into the revenge. Aegisthus must be killed in a specific place, "the spot / where you slaughtered my father" (1986–87). Orestes pursues the issue of justice:

AEGISTHUS You lead the way.

ORESTES No you go first.

AEGISTHUS Afraid I'll escape?

ORESTES You shall not die on your own terms.
I will make it bitter for you.　　　　(1995–99)

It has been suggested that in these lines Orestes is trying to make the punishment unpleasant in every way (so Jebb), or even that he is torturing Aegisthus.[37] However, the amount of pain involved here is so minute that Orestes must have some purpose other than making Aegisthus' death unpleasant. Since Orestes has just said that Aegisthus must die in the same place where he killed Agamemnon, it seems likely that here, too, he is trying to give this action the character of a just punishment.[38] If reciprocity is the principle involved, then it must be so that Aegisthus' death will resemble that of Agamemnon by being

36. Reinhardt, (note 24, above) page 138.
37. So Kells, note on line 1503.
38. Orestes in Aeschylus' version also stresses proportionality when he says to Clytemnestra: "you killed one whom you should not have; now suffer that which you should not" (*Libation Bearers*, 930).

not what he wanted. However, it is also possible that Orestes is making certain that Aegisthus dies against his will, to preserve the quality of a punishment.

Orestes' final lines, on the other hand, seem to be clearly flawed:

> And let such judgment fall
> on any who wish to break the law:
> kill them!   (2000–2002)

Despite the crudity of Orestes' logic, it contains the concept of equity. It was a feature of the archaic laws of Drakon that every crime was punished by death, and it may be that what the first audience heard in Orestes' final lines is a primitive justice.

Electra and Orestes have played their parts well, but they do not fully understand what they have done, nor have they remained unmarked by violence. Electra has achieved near divine status in her martyrdom to right conduct, but she frequently errs when she speaks about the nature of justice and of just process. One of the main reasons Aegisthus should die is to relieve her of the sight of him, but he should be allowed to speak and should not be thrown to the dogs. Orestes is true to the letter of Apollo's oracle, by employing the trick, but also to the spirit of that oracle, by injecting proportionality into the punishment where he can. On the other hand, he has no inkling of the justice that will emerge when he goes to Athens to stand trial.

The chorus end the play with a careful statement, in its way as limited as those of Electra when she said that Aegisthus' murder is the release of pains for her:

> O seed of Atreus:
> you suffered and broke free . . .   (2004–5)

This seems to me to be true. No matter what Orestes suffers for killing his mother, he is a free man, in control, restored to his proper status; this also implies that the legitimate will inherit in the future. That is what I take it to mean when they say to the seed of Atreus, in their final line,

> you have won your way through
> to the finish.   (2007–8)

Orestes is "the seed," but it is also true that "the seed" is the process of legitimate inheritance—only when legitimate inheritance exists is the seed really a seed. They do not say that the future will be without trouble, any more than Electra did. The substantial accomplishment here is that Argos and the house of Atreus are "free." Thus Electra's word, "release," is apt—the mood of the end of the play is the mood of release.

We should not underestimate this mood of release. That this play is about a horrible act is indubitable, but it is also about the death of tyrants. Their rule rested on force and nothing else. And the chorus's reference to freedom and order restored is of transcendent importance. On at least one occasion, a performance of this play turned into a celebration of democracy. The Greek of the chorus's final lines contains the word "freedom." When I saw this play in Athens in the early 1970s, under the reign of the Colonels, after the play ended the crowd began to chant, "freedom, freedom." Men in military uniform scuttled out of the theater. Roses rained down on the actress who had portrayed Electra.

Lawrence, Kansas
2000

MICHAEL SHAW

TRANSLATOR'S FOREWORD

Screaming in Translation: The *Electra* of Sophocles

And how the red wild sparkles dimly burn
Through the ashen grayness.
      ELIZABETH BARRETT BROWNING

A translator is someone trying to get in between a body and its shadow. Translating is a task of imitation that faces in two directions at once, for it must line itself up with the solid body of the original text and at the same time with the shadow of that text where it falls across another language. Shadows fall and move. The following paper, based on my own attempts to render the Greek text of Sophocles' *Electra* into English, will indicate some of the moving shadows cast by this unusual and difficult play and describe how they have proven problematic for its translation into readable verse and performable drama.[1]

First I will consider screaming. Because the presence in Greek drama of bursts of sound expressing strong emotion (like OIMOI or O TALAINA or PHEU PHEU) furnishes the translator with a very simple and intractable problem. It has been generally assumed that they represent a somewhat formulaic body of ejaculatory utterance best rendered into English by some dead phrase like Alas! or Woe is me! But I discovered when studying the language of Electra that her screams are far from formulaic. They contribute to her characterization as creatively as many other aspects of her diction.

Electra's diction, especially her verbs, is the second topic I will discuss. There is one particular verb, repeated seven times in the play, with which Sophocles takes linguistic risks that have no synonym in English. It is a verb that means 'to cause pain' and Electra uses it in

---

1. I am grateful to Francis Dunn (then) of Northwestern University in Chicago (now UC Santa Barbara), who gave me the opportunity to present this paper at the symposium *Sophocles' Electra: Greek Tragedy In Word And Action* cosponsored by the Departments of Classics and Theatre in May 1993. Greek texts are cited from the edition of Sir Richard Jebb, Cambridge, 1894. Works consulted include the translation of D. Grene in *Sophocles II*, Chicago, 1957, the commentary of J. C. Kamerbeek, Leiden, 1974, the edition of R. H. Mather 1889, and the translation of Ezra Pound and R. Flemming, New York, 1990.

unique ways. The uniqueness of Electra's pain emerges not only from her diction but also musically. Thirdly and very briefly I will discuss the verbal and rhythmic music of Electra, especially in her interactions with the chorus in the opening movement of the play.

Screaming is a fairly typical activity of characters in Greek drama. But it was Virginia Woolf who noticed, perhaps after a night of listening to the birds in her garden talking ancient Greek, that there is something original about the screaming of Sophocles' Electra. In her essay on this play in *The Common Reader* Virginia Woolf says:[2]

> . . . his Electra stands before us like a figure so tightly bound that she can only move an inch this way, an inch that. But each movement must tell to the utmost, or . . . she will be nothing but a dummy, tightly bound. Her words in crisis are, as a matter of fact, bare; mere cries of despair, joy, hate . . . But it is not so easy to decide what it is that gives these cries of Electra in her anguish their power to cut and wound and excite.

Indeed it is not easy to decide what gives the screaming of Electra its power. Sophocles has invented for her a language of lament that is like listening to an X-ray. Electra's cries are just bones of sound. I itemize the cries of Electra as follows:

1. O
2. IO
3. PHEU
4. AIAI
5. TALAINA
6. OIMOI MOI
7. IO MOI MOI
8. EE IO
9. EE AIAI
10. IO GONAI
11. OIMOI TALAINA
12. OI 'GO TALAINA
13. OTOTOTOTOI TO TOI
14. IO MOI MOI DYSTENOS

In range and diversity of aural construction Electra surpasses all other screamers in Sophocles, including Philoctetes who suffers from gangrene in the foot and Heracles who gets burned alive at the end of his play. Let us consider how Electra constructs her screams. It should be noted at the outset that none of them occur extra metrum: they scan, and are to be taken as integral to the rhythmic and musical economy of her utterance. As units of sound they employ the usual features of

2. London, 1925, p. 26.

ritual lament (assonance, alliteration, internal rhyme, balance, symmetry, repetition)[3] in unusual ways. She creates, for example, certain unpronounceable concatenations of hiatus like EE AIAI or EE IO which hold the voice and the mouth open for the whole length of a measure of verse and are as painful to listen to as they are to say. The effect of such sounds is well described by Electra herself at 242–3, where she refers to her own language of lament in the phrase:

hiatus

pterygas/ oxytonôn goôn
πτέρυγας / ὀξυτόνων γόων

literally, "wings of sharpstretched laments" or "wings of screamings that are strained to sharp points." The phrase in Greek undulates harshly, onomatopoeic of the cries themselves. But it has also an image of straining or stretching—the straining of sound and emotion against enclosing limits—which is important to the concept of the whole passage. Electra here is talking about the evil of the house of Atreus as if it were a trap that has closed around her life. She believes that nothing except her voice can penetrate the walls of this enclosure. "My cries are wings, they pierce the cage," is how I translated the verse, losing the sound effect of the Greek but retaining the aggressivity of the cries and also the terrible sense of stuckness that characterizes Electra's self-descriptions. For example at v. 132f. she summarizes her own stuck situation in the double negative construction:

oud' ethelô . . . / mê ou . . . stenachein
οὐδ᾽ ἐθέλω . . . / μὴ οὐ . . . στενάχειν
"I cannot *not* grieve . . ."

This same stuckness informs certain of the screams of Electra, for example the strangely compressed *oi 'go talaina*. This phrase is a three-part construction which combines the exclamation *oi* (conventionally translated "Alas!" or the like) with the first person singular pronoun *egô* ("I") and the standard adjective of tragic self-description *talaina* ("wretched, pitiable, miserable, sorry, sad, messed up"). These three components are forced together at high emotional pressure as if they formed a single entity of sound and self. It is an entity that elides Electra of part of her *egô*: the pronoun *egô* sacrifices its opening vowel to the encroachment of the exclamatory *oi* and then merges immediately with the epithet *talaina* so as to enclose Electra's

3. On characteristics of funeral lament, see M. Alexiou, *The Ritual Lament in Greek Tradition*, Cambridge, 1974.

egô in grief from both sides. As she says of herself at v. 147: "Grieving is a pattern that is cut and fitted around my mind" (*eme . . . araren phrenas*).

The mind of Electra is a remarkable machinery. It provides an unrelentingly lucid commentary on her stuck situation from the first moment she enters the stage. She begins the parodos, for example, by naming two other stuck people as paradigms for herself, Niobe who is literally petrified by grief for her dead children, and Procne who has been transformed into a nightingale by remorse for her dead son. But it is not their emotional paralysis that Electra venerates. For her, Niobe and Procne represent a victory of female sign language. They are women who have left behind human form and rational speech yet have not let go the making of meaning. The water that pours perpetually down Niobe's rock face, the twittering that pours perpetually from Procne's bird mouth, are analogues for Electra's private language of screams. Each of these three women manages to say what she means from within an idiolect that is alien or unknown to other people. Each of them manages, although stuck in a form of life that cuts her off from the world of normal converse, to transect and trouble and change that world by her utterance. Electra admires Niobe and Procne because each of them has a significatory power, as she does, herself, to sabotage the world of other people and normal converse.

Now Electra has a special verb for this action of sabotage, which she has come to regard as identical with her own function. It is the verb *lupein* and it figures in one of the strangest sentences of the play. The Greek lexicon defines *lupein* in the active as "to grieve, vex, cause pain, do harm, harass, distress, damage, violate" and in the passive as "to be vexed, violated, harassed," etc. or "to grieve, feel pain." The cognate noun *lupê* means "pain of body" or "pain of mind" or "sad plight." Electra uses this verb to assert her philosophy of action at v. 355, where she says that public lament is her whole function in life because by this action she can *lupein*—grieve, harass, distress, damage, violate— her mother. In the following verses she summarizes her philosophy of self in a sentence formed around this same verb *lupein*:

> emoi gar estô toume mê lupein monon / boskêma (363–4)
> ἐμοὶ γὰρ ἔστω τοὐμὲ μὴ λυπεῖν μόνον / βόσκημα
> ["For me yes let be not damaging me the only food."]

> "For me be it food enough that I do not wound mine own
> conscience." (R. C. Jebb)

> "For me let it be meat and drink not to put my self out."
> (R. H. Mather)

"All the food I need is the quiet of my conscience." (D. Grene)

"Keep my self-respect anyhow." (E. Pound)

During the days and weeks when I was working on this play I used to dream about translating. One night I dreamed that the text of the play was a big solid glass house. I floated above the house trying to zero in on v. 363. I was carrying in my hands wrapped in a piece of black cloth the perfect English equivalent for *lupein* and I kept trying to force myself down through the glass atmosphere of the house to position this word in its right place. But there was an upward pressure as heavy as water. I couldn't move down, I swam helplessly back and forth on the surface of the transparency, waving my black object and staring down at the text through fathoms of glass. And I was just about to take the black cloth off and look at the word so as to memorize it for later when I awoke, when I awoke.

I never did discover, asleep or awake, what was under that black cloth. I never did hit upon the right translation for *lupein*. But Electra's use of this verb (particularly at v. 363) continues to disturb me because of the way it sums her up. As Virginia Woolf says, "the stable, the permanent, the original human being is to be found there."[4] When we look at the syntax of v. 363 we see a sentence formed around a verb, the infinitive *lupein*, but the verb is made into a negative by the addition of the adverb *mê* ("to not vex, harm, damage, etc. . . .") and then the negatived verb is made into a noun by the addition of the article *to* ("the act of not vexing, harming, damaging, etc. . . ."). So too in Electra's life we see all positive action negatived by hatred and then this negative condition reified as personal destiny. Actionless she feeds on her own negativity. "It is the only Food that grows," as Emily Dickinson says of another equally private religion of pain.[5] This strange black food is named again by Electra, this time as a noun, at v. 822 in its full suicidal implication:

> lupê d' ean zô· tou biou d' oudeis pothos.
> λύπη δ' ἐὰν ζῶ τοῦ βίου δ' οὐδεὶς πόθος.
> "It is damage [pain, violation etc.] if I continue to exist.
> No desire for life [is in me]."

She expresses another death wish with the participle of the verb at v. 1170:

---

4. *The Common Reader* [n. 4, above], 27.
5. T. H. Johnson, ed., *The Complete Poems of Emily Dickinson*, Boston, 1890, # 1555.

> tous gar thanontas oukh horô lupoumenous.
> τοὺς γὰρ θανόντας οὐχ ὁρῶ λυπουμένους,
> "For the dead, I see, feel no pain."

Electra has a talent for brutal antithesis but these statements are not, I think, rhetorically formed. They touch a null point at the centre of the woman's soul. And they have the same X-ray quality as some of her screams.

But for the translator the problem presented by Electra's screams and diction in general is contextual. She uses fairly common verbs and nouns, and Sophocles goes out of his way to show us her X-ray utterances projected on the ordinary language screen of other people. This creates an especially jarring effect when we hear them using her words. For example when Orestes, dismissing the notion that lying and deceit are bad things, tosses off the phrase:

> ti gar me lupei touth' . . .
> τί γὰρ με λυπεῖ τοῦθ' . . .
> "What harm does this do me [to die in words
> if I am saved in fact]?"   (59–60)

In Orestes' much more lightly maintained moral order, Electra's black verb *lupei* is little more than a synonym for "What's the problem?" A similar shock effect is felt when we hear Clytemnestra appropriate Electra's noun *lupê* to denote pain of childbirth. Clytemnestra is referring to Agamemnon and Iphigeneia when she says (532–33),

> . . . ouk ison kamôn emoi / lupês, hot' espeir', hôsper hê tiktous' egô.
> . . . οὐκ ἴσον καμὼν ἐμοὶ / λύπης, ὅτ' ἔσπειρ', ὥσπερ ἡ τίκτουσ' ἐγώ.
> ". . . Did he have some share in the pain [*lupês*] of her birth? No! I
> did it myself."

This is one category of pain that the resolutely asexual Electra will never know, and furthermore, as she tells us repeatedly throughout the play, the very idea of genetic connexion or genital analogy between herself and her mother fills her with horror. "Mother she is called but mother she is not," Electra announces at one point to her sister. And although on one level Electra can be said to instantiate every girl's fear of turning into her mother, it is also true that in this case both the girl and the mother are prodigious—the mother for her shamelessness, the girl for her shame. It is not until we hear Clytemnestra decline Electra's word *lupê* to its most fleshly and female connotation that we understand Electra's shame in its full human and sexual aspect. There is something *unnatural*, something radical and alien, for Sophocles and his audience, about the way female shame has constructed around Electra a sort of life-size funeral urn which she inhabits as if it were a life.

Alienation is also indicated musically in the Sophoclean text. Electra's music is a standing discrepancy to tragic convention and other people's expectations. She takes over the stage musically from the first moment of her entrance—in fact from before her entrance, for the first sound Electra makes at v.77 interrupts the iambic procedure of the prologue with an offstage scream in what seems an aborted lyric anapaest. The monodic song of Electra that follows is intrusive in every way. It replaces the entrance song of the chorus which should occur at this point and usurps the anapaestic metre in which the chorus conventionally sing the entrance song. Rhetorically, Electra's monody rivals anything in Greek drama for the sheer egotism of its address. She begins by saying (86–87):

> ô phaos hagnon / kai gês isomoir' aêr . . .
> ὦ φάος ἁγνὸν / καὶ γῆς ἰσόμοιρ' ἀήρ . . .
> "O holy light and equal air shaped on the world . . ."

and goes on to call the entire cosmos to collaborate in her private drama of mourning and revenge. But the odd thing about this cosmic song is that it both begins and ends with a metaphor of measure. In the first verse (87) she measures air against earth with the phrase *gês isomoir' aêr*, and in the last verse she measures herself against the whole history of evil in the house of Atreus saying (119–20),

> mounê gar agein ouketi sôkô / lupês antirrhopon
>   achthos.
> μούνη γὰρ ἄγειν οὐκέτι σωκῶ / λύπης ἀντίρροπον ἄχθος.
> "Because alone the whole poised force of my life is
>   nothing against this pain."

It is typical of Sophoclean heroes to set for themselves cosmic parameters of moral action. By framing Electra in images of measure Sophocles reminds us that she is someone off the scale. And he is able to make this heroic discrepancy clear, in the long lyric interchange between Electra and the chorus that follows her monody, by a very simple musical effect.

The dramatic purpose of this interchange is to show Electra in interaction with a society sympathetic to her dilemma and realistic about her options. And moreover to show Electra, in the midst of such people, utterly alone. The antiphonal nature of the song emphasizes this.

Antiphony organizes the song into alternating strophes and antistrophes. Each strophic pair follows a principle of responsion whereby the first verse of the strophe responds metrically with the first verse of the antistrophe, the second verse with the second verse, and so on. This arrangement is generally used to create a lyric dialogue between two voices. If Electra and the chorus had sung strophe and antistrophe respectively, the effect would have been one of shared thought or interwoven emotion. But Sophocles has chosen to further subdivide each strophe and antistrophe so that each six lines of Electra respond with another six lines of Electra, each six lines of the chorus respond with another six lines of the chorus. They are each talking to themselves. Musically, it is an anti-dialogue.

Conceptually also. Each time the chorus talk they send a drift of platitudes down over Electra who knocks them away with one hand. Each choral utterance attempts to steer the discussion towards general truths and perspectives wider than the individual life. Electra keeps pulling the focus back to herself with a resolute first-person pronoun or verb. The chorus talk strategies for going on with life, Electra declares life an irrelevancy. It is death that absorbs Electra's whole imagination and the darkness that is soaking out of this one fact seems to colour the music and reasoning of everything she says in the song, especially when we see these continually measured against the bright banalities of the chorus. And at the point where Electra's anger and despair finally boil over (236) she throws the metaphor of measure back at the chorus with a question as jagged as a scream:

> kai ti metron kakotâtos ephu?
> καὶ τί μέτρον κακότατος ἔφυ;
> "And at what point does the evil level off in my life, tell me that!"

Nobody answers her.

ANNE CARSON

ELECTRA

CHARACTERS

PAEDAGOGUS OR OLD MAN servant and former tutor of Orestes

ORESTES son of Clytemnestra and Agamemnon, king of Argos

CHRYSOTHEMIS daughter of Clytemnestra and Agamemnon

ELECTRA daughter of Clytemnestra and Agamemnon

CLYTEMNESTRA Queen of Argos

AEGISTHUS paramour of Clytemnestra

CHORUS of Mycenaean women

PYLADES Orestes' silent friend

Line numbers in the right-hand margin of the text refer to the English translation only, and the Notes on the text at p. 113 are keyed to these lines. The bracketed line numbers in the running head lines refer to the Greek text.

Scene: at Mycenae before the palace of Agamemnon.

Enter the OLD MAN *and* ORESTES *with* PYLADES

PAEDAGOGUS You are his son! Your father
marshaled the armies at Troy once—
child of Agamemnon: look around you now.
Here is the land you were longing to see all that time.
Ancient Argos. You dreamed of this place.
The grove of Io, where the gadfly drove her.
Look, Orestes. There is the marketplace
named for Apollo,
wolfkiller god.
And on the left, the famous temple of Hera.   10
But stop! There—do you know what that is?
Mycenae. Yes. Look at it. Walls of gold!
Walls of death. It is the house of Pelops.
I got you out of there
out of the midst of your father's murder,
one day long ago.
From the hands of your sister
I carried you off. Saved your life. Reared you up—
to this: to manhood. To avenge your father's death.
So, Orestes! And you, dear   20
Pylades—
Now is the time to decide what to do.
Already the sun is hot upon us.
Birds are shaking, the world is awake.
Black stars and night have died away.
So before anyone is up and about
let's talk.
Now is no time to delay.
This is the edge of action.

ORESTES I love you, old man.   30
The signs of goodness shine from your face.
Like a thoroughbred horse—he gets old,

51

but he does not lose heart,
he pricks up his ears—so you
urge me forward
and stand in the front rank yourself.
Good. Now,
I will outline my plan. You
listen sharp.
If I'm off target anywhere,   40
set me straight.
You see, I went to Pytho
to ask the oracle how I could get justice
from the killers of my father.
Apollo answered:

Take no weapons.
No shield.
No army.
Go alone—a hand in the night.
Snare them.   50
Slaughter them.
You have the right.

That is the oracle.
Here is the plan:
you go into the house at the first chance.
Find out all that is happening there.
Find out and report to us. Be very clear.
You're so old, they won't know you.
And your garlands will fool them.
Now this is your story: 60
you're a stranger from Phocis,
from the house of Phanoteus
(he's the most powerful ally they have).
Tell them on oath that Orestes is dead.
An accident. Fatal:
rolled out of his chariot on the racetrack at Delphi.
Dragged to death under the wheels.
Let that be the story.
Meanwhile, we go to my father's grave,
as Apollo commanded,   70
to pour libation and crown the tomb
with locks of hair cut from my head.

Then we'll be back
with that bronzeplated urn
(you know, the one I hid in the bushes).
Oh yes, we'll fool them
with this tale of me dead,
burnt,
nothing left but ash.
What good news for them!   80

As for me—
what harm can it do
to die in words?
I save my life and win glory besides!
Can a mere story be evil? No, of course not—
so long as it pays in the end.
I know of shrewd men
who die a false death
so as to come home
all the more valued.   90
Yes, I am sure:
I will stand clear of this lie
and break on my enemies like a star.

O land of my fathers! O gods of this place!
Take me in. Give me luck on this road.
House of my father:
I come to cleanse you with justice.
I come sent by gods.
Do not exile me from honor!
Put me in full command   100
of the wealth and the house!
Enough talk.
Old man, look to your task.
We are off.
This is the point on which everything hinges.
This is the moment of proof.

ELECTRA   *A cry from inside the house* IO MOI MOI DYSTENOS.

OLD MAN What was that? I heard
         a cry—some servant in the house?

ORESTES Can it be poor Electra?   110
        Should we stay here and listen?

OLD MAN No. Nothing precedes the work of Apollo.
        That is our first step: your father's libations.
        That is the way to win: action.

                Exit OLD MAN *and* ORESTES *with* PYLADES. *Enter* ELECTRA
                                            from the palace.

ELECTRA O holy light!
        And equal air shaped on the world—
        you hear my songs,
        you hear the blows fall.
        You know the blood runs
        when night sinks away.   120
        All night I watch.
        All night I mourn,
        in this bed that I hate in this house I detest.
        How many times can a heart break?
        Oh father,
        it was not killer Ares
        who opened his arms
        in some foreign land
        to welcome you.
        But my own mother and her lover Aegisthus: 130
        those two good woodsmen
        took an axe and split you down like an oak.
        No pity for these things,
        there is no pity
        but mine,
        oh father,
        for the pity of your butchering rawblood death.

        Never
        will I leave off lamenting,
        never. No.   140
        As long as the stars sweep through heaven.
        As long as I look on this daylight.
        No.
        Like the nightingale who lost her child
        I will stand in his doorway

and call on his name.
Make them all hear.
Make this house echo.
O Hades!
Persephone!   150
Hermes of hell!
Furies, I call you!
Who watch
when lives are murdered.
Who watch when loves betray.
Come! Help me! Strike back!
Strike back for my father murdered!
And send my brother to me.
Because
alone,   160
the whole poised force of my life is nothing
against this.

Enter CHORUS

CHORUS Your mother is evil   *strophe* 1
        but oh my child why
        melt your life away in mourning?
        Why let grief eat you alive?
        It was long ago
        she took your father:
        her hand came out of unholy dark
        and cut him down.   170
        I curse the one
        who did the deed
        (if this is right to say).

ELECTRA You are women of noble instinct
        and you come to console me
        in my pain.
        I know.
        I do understand.
        But I will not let go this man or this mourning.

        He is my father.   180
        I cannot not grieve.
        Oh my friends,

Friendship is a tension. It makes delicate demands.
I ask this one thing:
[let me go mad in my own way.]

antistrophe 1

CHORUS Not from Hades' black and universal lake can you lift
     him.
  not by groaning, not by prayers.
  Yet you run yourself out
  in a grief with no cure,
  no time-limit, no measure.   190
  It is a knot no one can untie.
  Why are you so in love with
  things unbearable?

ELECTRA None but a fool or an infant
  could forget a father
  gone so far and cold.
  No.
  Lament is a pattern cut and fitted around my mind—
  like the bird who calls Itys! Itys! endlessly,
  bird of grief,   200
  angel of Zeus.
  O heartdragging Niobe,
  I count you a god:
  buried in rock yet
  always you weep.

CHORUS You are not the only one in the world   *strophe* 2
  my child, who has stood in the glare of grief.
  Compare yourself:
  you go too far.
  Look at your sister, Chrysothemis: 210
  she goes on living. So does Iphianassa.
  And the boy—his secret years are sorrowful too,
  but he will be brilliant
  one day when Mycenae welcomes him home
  to his father's place, to his own land
  in the guidance of Zeus—
  Orestes!

ELECTRA Him yes!
I am past exhaustion
in waiting for him—   220
no children,
no marriage,
no light in my heart.
I live in a place of tears.
And he
simply forgets.
Forgets what he suffered,
forgets what he knew.
Messages reach me, each one belied.
He is passionate—as any lover.   230
But his passion does not bring him here.

CHORUS Have courage,   *antistrophe 2*
my child.
Zeus is still great in heaven,
he watches and governs all things.
Leave this anger to Zeus: it burns too high in you.
Don't hate so much.
Nor let memory go.
For time is a god who can simplify all.
And as for Orestes   240
on the shore of Crisa·
where oxen graze—
he does not forget you.
Nor is the king of death
on the banks of Acheron
unaware.

ELECTRA But meanwhile most of my life has slid by
without hope.
I sink.
I melt.   250
Father has gone and there is no man left
who cares enough to stand up for me.
Like some beggar
wandered in off the street,
I serve as a slave
in the halls of my father.

Dressed in these rags,
I stand at the table
and feast on air.

CHORUS One rawblood cry   *strophe 3*   260
        on the day he returned,
        one rawblood cry went through the halls
        just as the axeblade
        rose
        and fell.
        He was caught by guile,
        cut down by lust:
        together they bred a thing shaped like a monster—
        god or mortal
        no one knows.   270

ELECTRA That day tore out the nerves of my life.
         That night:
         far too silent the feasting,
         much too sudden
         the silence.
         My father looked up and saw
         death coming out of their hands.
         Those hands took my life hostage.
         Those hands murdered me.
         I pray   280
         the great god of Olympus
         give them pain on pain to pay for this!
         And smother the glow
         of deeds like these.

CHORUS Think again, Electra.   *antistrophe 3*
        Don't say any more.
        Don't you see what you're doing?
        you make your own pain.
        Why keep wounding yourself?
        With so much evil stored up   290
        in that cold dark soul of yours

        you breed enemies everywhere you touch.
        But you must not
        clash with the people in power.

ELECTRA By dread things I am compelled. I know that.
         I see the trap closing.
         I know what I am.
         But while life is in me
         I will not stop this violence. No.
         Oh my friends   300
         who is there to comfort me?
         Who understands?
         Leave me be,
         let me go,
         do not soothe me.
         This is a knot no one can untie.
         There will be no rest,
         there is no retrieval.
         No number exists for
         griefs like these.   310

CHORUS   Yes but I speak from concern—   *epode*
         as a mother would: trust me.
         Do not breed violence out of violence.

ELECTRA Alright then, you tell me one thing—
         at what point does the evil level off in my life?
         You say ignore the deed—is that right?
         Who could approve this?
         It defies human instinct!
         Such ethics make no sense to me.
         And how could I nestle myself in a life of ease   320

         while my father lies out in the cold,
         outside honor?
         My cries are wings:
         they pierce the cage.
         For if a dead man is earth and nothing,
         if a dead man is void and dead space lying,
         if a dead man's murderers
         do not give
         blood for blood
         to pay for this,   330

then shame does not exist.
Human reverence
is gone.

CHORUS I came here, child, because I care
for your welfare as my own.
But perhaps I am wrong.
Let it be as you say.

ELECTRA Women, I am ashamed before you: I know
you find me extreme
in my grief.   340
I bear it hard.
But I tell you I have no choice.
It compels. I act because it compels.
Oh forgive me. But how could I—
how could a woman of any nobility
stand
and watch her father's house go bad?
There is something bad here,
growing. Day and night
I watch it. Growing.   350

My mother is where it begins.
She and I are at war.
Our relation is hatred.
And I live in this house
with my father's own killers:
they rule me. They dole out my life.
What kind of days do you think I have here?
I see my father's throne
with Aegisthus on it.
I see my father's robes   360
with Aegisthus in them.
I see my father's hearth with Aegisthus presiding—
right where he stood when he struck
my father down!
And the final outrage:
the killer tucked in my father's bed.
Behold the man who pleasures my mother—
should I call that thing 'mother' that lies at his side?
God! Her nerve astounds me.

She lives with that polluted object,   370
fearing no fury. No,
she laughs!
Celebrates
that day—the day she took my father
with dances and song and slaughter of sheep!
A monthly bloodgift to the gods who keep her safe.

I watch
all going dark in the rooms of my house.
I weep.
I melt.   380

I grieve
for the strange cruel feast made in my father's name.
But I grieve to myself:
not allowed even to shed the tears I would.
No—that creature
who calls herself noble
will shriek at me:
"Godcursed! You piece of hatred!
So you've lost your father—is that unique?
No mortal mourns but you?   390
Damn you.
May the gods of hell damn you
to groan perpetually there
as you groan
perpetually
here!"
That's her style—
and when she hears someone mention Orestes,
then she goes wild, comes screaming at me:
"Have I you to thank for this?   400

Isn't it your work? Wasn't it you
who stole Orestes out of my hands
and smuggled him away?
You'll pay for it.
I tell you, you will pay."
Howling bitch. And by her side
the brave bridegroom—
this lump of bad meat.

With women only
he makes his war.   410

And I wait.
I wait.
I wait
for Orestes.
He will come! He will end this.
But my life is dying out.
He is always on the verge of doing something
then does nothing.
He has worn out all the hopes I had or could have.
Oh my friends,   420
in times like these,
self-control has no meaning.
Rules of reverence do not apply.
Evil is a pressure that shapes us to itself.

CHORUS   Is Aegisthus at home?

ELECTRA   No. Do you think I'd be
standing outdoors?
He is gone to the fields.

CHORUS   That gives me courage
to say what I came to say.   430

ELECTRA   What is it you want?

CHORUS   I want to know—your brother—
do you say he is coming? Or has a plan?

ELECTRA   Yes, he says so. But he says a lot. Does nothing.

CHORUS   A man who does a great deed may hesitate.

ELECTRA   Oh? I saved his life without hesitating.

CHORUS   Courage. His nature is good, he will not fail his kin.

ELECTRA   That belief is what keeps me alive.

CHORUS Quiet now. Here is your sister come from the house,
Chrysothemis, of the same father   440
and mother as you.
She has offerings in her hands,
as if for the dead.

Enter CHRYSOTHEMIS *carrying garlands and a vessel*

CHRYSOTHEMIS Here you are again at the doorway, sister,
telling your tale to the world!
When will you learn?
It's pointless. Pure self-indulgence.
Yes, I know how bad things are.
I suffer too — if I had the strength
I would show what I think of them.   450
But now is not the right time.
In rough waters, lower the sail, is my theory.
Why pretend to be doing,
unless I can do some real harm?
I wish you would see this.
And yet,
it is true,
justice is not on my side.
Your choice is the right one. On the other hand,
if I want to live a free woman,   460
there are masters who must be obeyed.

ELECTRA You appall me.
Think of the father who sired you! But you do not.
All your thought is for her.
These sermons you give me are all learnt
from mother, not a word is your own.
Well it's time for you to make a choice:
quit being 'sensible'
or keep your good sense and betray your own kin.
Wasn't it you who just said,   470
"If I had the strength I would show how I hate them!"
Yet here I am doing everything possible
to avenge our father,
and do you help? No!
You try to turn me aside.

Isn't this simply cowardice added to evil?
Instruct me—no! Let me tell you:
what do I stand to gain if I cease my lament?
Do I not live? Badly, I know, but I live.
What is more,   480
I am a violation to them.
And so, honor the dead—
if any grace exists down there.
Now
you hate them, you say.
But this hate is all words.
In fact, you live with the killers.
And I tell you,
if someone were to give me
all the gifts that make your days delicious,   490
I would not bend. No.
You can have your rich table
and life flowing over the cup.
I need one food:
I must not violate Electra.
As for your status, I couldn't care less.
Nor would you, if you had any self-respect.
You could have been called
child of the noblest men!
Instead they call you mother's girl,   500
they think you base.
Your own dead father,
your own loved ones,
you do betray.

CHORUS No anger I pray.
There is profit for both
if you listen to one another.

CHRYSOTHEMIS Her talk is no surprise to me, ladies.
I'm used to this.
And I wouldn't have bothered   510
to speak at all, except—
for the rumor I heard.
There is very great evil coming this way,
something to cut her long laments
short.

ELECTRA Tell me what is the terrible thing?
         If it is worse than my present life,
         I give up.

CHRYSOTHEMIS I tell what I know:
              they plan,   520
              unless you cease from this mourning,
              to send you where you will not see the sun again.
              You'll be singing your songs
              alive
              in a room
              in the ground.
              Think about that.
              And don't blame me when you suffer.
              Too late then.
              Now is the time to start being sensible.   530

ELECTRA Ah. That is their intention, is it.

CHRYSOTHEMIS It is. As soon as Aegisthus comes home.

ELECTRA May he come soon, then.

CHRYSOTHEMIS What are you saying?

ELECTRA Let him come, if he has his plan ready.

CHRYSOTHEMIS What do you mean? Are you losing your mind?

ELECTRA I want to escape from you all.

CHRYSOTHEMIS Not go on living?

ELECTRA Living? Oh yes
         my life is a beautiful thing, is it not.   540

CHRYSOTHEMIS Well it could be, if you got some sense.

ELECTRA Don't bother telling me to betray those I love.

CHRYSOTHEMIS I tell you we have masters, we must bend.

ELECTRA *You* bend—you go ahead and lick their boots.
It's not my way.

CHRYSOTHEMIS Don't ruin your life in sheer stupidity.

ELECTRA I will ruin my life, if need be,
avenging our father.

CHRYSOTHEMIS But our father, I know, forgives us for this.

ELECTRA Cowards' talk.   550

CHRYSOTHEMIS You won't listen to reason at all, will you?

ELECTRA No. My mind is my own.

CHRYSOTHEMIS Well then I'll be on my way.

ELECTRA Where are you going? Whose offerings are those?

CHRYSOTHEMIS Mother is sending me to father's tomb,
to pour libation.

ELECTRA What? To her mortal enemy?

CHRYSOTHEMIS To her 'murder victim,' as you like to say.

ELECTRA Whose idea was this?

CHRYSOTHEMIS It came out of a dream in the night, I believe.   560

ELECTRA Gods of my father be with me now!

CHRYSOTHEMIS You take courage from a nightmare?

ELECTRA Tell the dream and I'll answer you.

CHRYSOTHEMIS There is little to tell.

ELECTRA Tell it anyway.
Little words can mean
death or life sometimes.

CHRYSOTHEMIS Well the story is
                  she dreamed of our father
                  and knew him again   570
                  for he came back into the light.
                  Then she saw him take hold of his sceptre
                  and stick it in the hearth—
                  his own sceptre from the old days,
                  that Aegisthus carries now.
                  And from the sceptre sprang a branch
                  in full climbing leaf
                  which cast a shadow over the whole land of Mycenae.
                  That is as much as I got
                  from one who overheard her   580
                  telling the dream to the sun.
                  More I don't know, except
                  fear is her reason for sending me out today.
                  So I beg you, by the gods of our family,
                  listen to me.
                  Don't throw your life away on plain stupidity.
                  For if you spurn me now,
                  you'll come begging later
                  when the trouble starts.

ELECTRA Oh dear one, no.   590
             You cannot touch this tomb
             with any of those things you have in your hands.
             It breaks the law. It would be unholy
             to bring that woman's libations
             to our father: she is the enemy.
             No. Pitch them to the winds
             or down a dark hole.
             They shall come nowhere near his resting place.
             But when she dies and goes below,
             she will find them waiting.   600
             Treasure keeps, down there.

             God! Her nerve is astounding.
             What woman alive would send gifts
             to garnish her own murder victim?
             And do you imagine
             the dead man would welcome such
             honors

from the hand of the woman who butchered him—
think! To clean her blade she wiped it off on his head!
You astonish me—do you really believe   610
such gifts will cancel murder?
Throw them away.
Here, instead
cut a lock from your hair
and a lock of mine—meagre gifts
but it is all I have.
Take this to him, the hair
and this belt of mine,
though it's nothing elaborate.
Kneel down there and pray to him.   620
Pray he come up from the ground
to stand with us against our enemies.
Pray that his son Orestes live
to trample his enemies underfoot.
And someday you and I will go in better style than this
to crown his tomb.
But I wonder. You know
I wonder—
suppose he had some part
in sending her these cold unlucky dreams.   630

Well, never mind that.
Sister,
do this deed.
Stand up for yourself
and for me and for this man we love
more than anyone else in the world,
this dead man. Your father. My father.

CHORUS   The girl speaks for human reverence.
And you,
if you have any sense, will do what she says.   640

CHRYSOTHEMIS   I will do it. It is the right thing,
why dispute?
But please, my friends,
I need silence from you.
if my mother finds out,

the attempt will turn bitter for me,
I fear.

Exit CHRYSOTHEMIS

CHORUS   Unless I am utterly wrong in my reading of omens   *strophe*
unless I am out of my mind
Justice is coming   650
with clear signs before her
and righteousness in her hands.
She is coming down on us, child, coming now!
There is courage
whispering into me
when I hear tell of these sweetbreathing dreams.
He does not forget—
the one who begot you
the king of the Greeks.
She does not forget—   660
the jaw that bit him in two:
ancient and sharpened on both sides to butcher the meat!

Vengeance is coming—her hands like an army   *antistrophe*
her feet as a host.
She will come out of hiding
come scorching down
on love that is filth
and beds that are blood
where marriage should never have happened!
Conviction   670
is strong in me:
visions like these are no innocent sign for killers.
I say no omens exist
for mortals to read
from the cold faces of dreams
or from oracles
unless this fragment of death steps into the daylight.

O horserace of Pelops,   *epode*
once long ago
you came in the shape of a wide calamity   680

to this land.
And from the time when

69

Myrtilus pitched and sank in the sea
his solid gold life
sliced off at the roots—
never
since that time
has this house
got itself clear of
rawblood   690
butchery.

Enter CLYTEMNESTRA

CLYTEMNESTRA Prowling the streets again, are you?
Of course, with Aegisthus away.
He was always the one
who kept you indoors where you couldn't embarrass us.
Now that he's gone you pay no heed to me.
Yet you love to make me the text of your lectures:
What an arrogant bitchminded tyrant I am,
a living insult to you and your whole way of being!
But do I in fact insult you? No. I merely return   700
the muck you throw at me.
Father, father, father! your perpetual excuse—
your father got his death from me. From me! That's right!
I make no denial.
It was Justice who took him, not I alone.
And you should have helped if you had any conscience.
For this father of yours,
this one you bewail,
this unique Greek,
had the heart to sacrifice your own sister to the gods. 710

And how was that? Did he have some share
in the pain of her birth? No—I did it myself!
Tell me:
why did he cut her throat? What was the reason?
You say for the Argives?
But they had no business to kill what was mine.
To save Menelaus?
Then I deserved recompense, wouldn't you say?
Did not Menelaus have children himself—
in fact two of them,   720

who ought to have died before mine
in all fairness?
Their mother, let's not forget,
was the cause of the whole expedition!
Or was it that Hades conceived some peculiar desire
to feast on my children instead?
Or perhaps
that murdering thug your father,
simply overlooked my children
in his tender care for Menelaus'.   730
Was that not brutal? Was that not perverse?

I say it was.
No doubt you disagree.
But I tell you one thing, that murdered girl
would speak for me if she had a voice.
Anyway, the deed is done.
I feel no remorse.
you think me degenerate?
Here's my advice:
perfect yourself   740
before you blame others.

ELECTRA At least you can't say I started it this time;
these ugly remarks are unprovoked.
But I want to get a few things clear
about the dead man and my sister as well.
If you allow me.

CLYTEMNESTRA Go ahead, by all means. Begin this way more often
and we won't need ugly remarks at all, will we?

ELECTRA All right then. Yes.
You killed my father, you admit.   750
What admission could bring more shame?
Never mind if it was legal or not—did you care?
Let's talk facts: there was only one reason you killed him.
You were seduced by that creature you live with.
Ask Artemis,
goddess of hunters,
why she stopped the winds at Aulis.
No, I'll tell you:

my father one day, so I hear,
was out in the grove of the goddess.   760
The sound of his footfall startled a stag out from cover
and, when he killed it, he let fall a boast.
This angered the daughter of Leto.
She held the Achaeans in check until,
as payment for the animal,
my father should offer his own daughter.
Hence, the sacrifice. There was no other way.
He had to free the army,
to sail home or towards Troy.
These were the pressures that closed upon him.   770

He resisted, he hated it—
and then he killed her.
Not for Menelaus' sake, no, not at all.
But even if—let's say we grant your claim—
he did these things to help his brother,
was it right he should die for it at your hands?
By what law?
Watch out: this particular law
could recoil upon your own head.
If we made it a rule   780
to answer killing with killing,
you would die first,
in all justice.
Open your eyes! The claim is a fake.
Tell me:
why do you live this way?
Your life is filth.
You share your bed with a bloodstained man:
once he obliged you by killing my father,
now you put him to use making children.   790
Once you had *decent* children from a *decent* father,
now you've thrown them out.
Am I supposed to praise that?
Or will you say
you do all this to avenge your child?
The thought is obscene—
to bed your enemies
and use a daughter as an alibi!
Oh why you go on? I can't argue with you.

You have your one same answer ready: 800
'That's no way to talk to your mother!'

Strange.
I don't think of you as mother at all.
You are some sort of punishment cage
locked around my life.
Evils from you, evils from him
are the air I breathe.
And what of Orestes?—he barely escaped you.
Poor boy.
The minutes are grinding him away somewhere.   810
You always accuse me
of training him up to be an avenger—

Oh I would if I could, you're so right!
Proclaim it to all!

Call me
baseminded, blackmouthing bitch! if you like—
for if this is my nature
we know how I come by it, don't we?

CHORUS   (*looking at Clytemnestra*)

Look. Anger is breathing out of her.
Yet she seems not to care   820
about right and wrong.

CLYTEMNESTRA Right and wrong!
What use is that in dealing with her?
Do you hear her insults?
And this girl is old enough to know better.
The fact is, she would do *anything*,
don't you see that?
No shame at all.

ELECTRA Ah now there you mistake me.
Shame I do feel.   830
And I know there is something all wrong about me—
believe me. Sometimes I shock myself.

But there is a reason: you.
You never let up
this one same pressure of hatred on my life:
I am the shape you made me.
Filth teaches filth.

CLYTEMNESTRA You little animal.
I and my deeds and my words draw
far too much comment from you.   840

ELECTRA You said it, not I.
For the deeds are your own.
But deeds find words for themselves,
don't they?

CLYTEMNESTRA By Artemis I swear, you will pay for this
when Aegisthus comes home!

ELECTRA See? You're out of control.
Though you gave me permission to say what I want,
you don't know how to listen.

CLYTEMNESTRA Silence! If you allow me   850
I will proceed with my sacrifice.
You spoke your piece.

ELECTRA Please! By all means! Go to it.
Not another word from me.

CLYTEMNESTRA (to her attendant) You there! Yes you—lift up
these offerings for me.
I will offer prayers to this our king
and loosen the fears that hold me now.
Do you hear me, Apollo?
I call you my champion!   860
But my words are guarded, for I am not among friends.
It wouldn't do to unfold the whole tale
with her standing here.
She has a destroying tongue in her
and she does love
to sow wild stories all over town.

So listen, I'll put it this way:
last night was a night of bad dreams
and ambiguous visions.
If they bode well for me, Lycian king, bring them to pass.   870
Otherwise, roll them back on my enemies!
And if there are certain people around
plotting to pull me down
from the wealth I enjoy,
do not allow it.
I want everything to go on as it is,
untroubled.
It suits me—this grand palace life
in the midst of my loved ones
and children—at least the ones   880
who do not bring me hatred and pain.

These are my prayers, Apollo.
Hear them.
Apollo,
grant them.
Gracious to all of us as we petition you.
And for the rest, though I keep silent,
I credit you with knowing it fully.
You are a god.
It goes without saying,   890
the children of Zeus see all things.
Amen.

                                        Enter OLD MAN

OLD MAN Ladies, can you tell me for certain
         if this is the house of Aegisthus the king?

CHORUS Yes, stranger, it is.

OLD MAN And am I correct that this is his wife?
         She has a certain royal look.

CHORUS Yes. That's who she is.

OLD MAN Greetings, queen. I have come with glad tidings
         for you and Aegisthus, from a friend of yours.   900

CLYTEMNESTRA That's welcome news. But tell me
              who sent you.

OLD MAN Phanoteus the Phocian. On a mission of some
         importance.

CLYTEMNESTRA What mission? Tell me.
              Insofar as I like Phanoteus,
              I am likely to like your news.

OLD MAN Orestes is dead. That is the sum of it.

ELECTRA OI 'GO TALAINA.
         My death begins now.

CLYTEMNESTRA What are you saying, what are you saying?   910
              Don't bother with her.

OLD MAN Orestes — dead. I say it again.

ELECTRA I am at the end. I exist no more.

CLYTEMNESTRA (to ELECTRA) Mind your own affairs, girl.
              But you, stranger — tell me the true story:
              how did he die?

OLD MAN Yes I was sent for this purpose, I'll tell the whole thing.
         Well:
         he had gone to the spectacle at Delphi,
         where all Greece turns up for the games.   920
         Things were just beginning to get under way
         and the herald's voice rang out
         announcing the footrace — first contest.
         When he came onto the track
         he was radiant. Every eye turned.
         Well, he leveled the competition,
         took first prize and came away famous.
         Oh there's so much to tell —
         I never saw anything like his performance! — but

let me come straight to the point.   930
He won every contest the judges announced—
single lap, double lap, pentathlon, you name it.

First prize every time.
He was beginning to take on an aura.
His name rang out over the track again and again:
"Argive Orestes,
whose father commanded the armies of Greece!"
So far so good.
But when a god sends harm,
no man can sidestep it,   940
no matter how strong he may be.
Came another day.
Sunrise: the chariot race.
He entered the lists.
What a pack:
there was one from Achaea,
a Spartan,
two Libyan drivers,
and he in the midst on Thessalian horses
stood fifth.   950
Sixth an Aetolian man, driving bays.
Seventh someone from Magnesia.
An Aenian man, riding white horses, had eighth place
and ninth a driver from godbuilt Athens.
Then a Boeotian.
Ten cars in all.
As they took their positions,
the judges cast lots to line up the cars.
A trumpet blast sounded.
They shot down the track.   960
All shouting together, reins tossing—

a hard clatter filled the whole course
and a vast float of dust,
as they all streamed together,
each one lashing and straining ahead
to the next axle box, the next snorting lip,
and the horse-foam flying
back over shoulders and wheels as they pounded past.
Meanwhile Orestes

just grazing the post each time with his wheel,   970
was letting his right horse go wide,
reining back on the other.
The cars were all upright at this point—

then all of a sudden
the Aenian's colts go out of control
and swerve off
just as they round the seventh turn.
They crash head-on into the Barcaean team.
Then one car after another comes ramming into the pile
and the whole plain of Crisa   980
fills with the smoke of wrecks.
Now
the Athenian driver was smart, he saw

what was happening.
Drew offside and waited as
the tide of cars went thundering by.
Orestes
was driving in last place,
lying back on his mares.
He had put his faith in the finish.   990
But as soon as he sees
the Athenian driver alone on the track

he lets out a cry that shivers his horses' ears
and goes after him.
Neck and neck
they are racing,
first one, then
the other
nosing ahead,
easing ahead.   1000

Now our unlucky boy had stood every course so far,
sailing right on in his upright car,
but at this point he lets the left rein go slack
with the horses turning,
he doesn't notice,
hits the pillar and
smashes the axle box in two.

Out he flips
over the chariot rail,
reins snarled around him   1010
and as he falls
the horses scatter midcourse.
They see him down. A gasp goes through the crowd:
"Not the boy!"
To go for glory and end like this—
pounded against the ground,
legs beating the sky—
the other drivers could hardly manage
to stop his team and cut him loose.
Blood everywhere.   1020
He was unrecognizable. Sickening.
They burned him at once on a pyre
and certain Phocians are bringing
the mighty body back—
just ashes,
a little bronze urn—
so you can bury him in his father's ground.
That is my story.
So far as words go,
gruesome enough.   1030
But for those who watched it,
and we did watch it,
the ugliest evil I ever saw.

CHORUS PHEU PHEU.
The whole ancient race
torn off at the roots. Gone.

CLYTEMNESTRA Zeus! What now? Should I call this good news?
Or a nightmare cut to my own advantage?
There is something grotesque
in having my own evils save my life.   1040

OLD MAN Why are you so disheartened at this news, my lady?

CLYTEMNESTRA To give birth is terrible, incomprehensible.
No matter how you suffer,
you cannot hate a child you've born.

OLD MAN My coming was futile then, it seems.

CLYTEMNESTRA Futile? Oh no. How—
if you've come with convincing proof of his death?
He was alive because I gave him life.
But he chose to desert my breasts and my care,
to live as an exile, aloof and strange.   1050
After he left here he never saw me.
But he laid against me
the death of his father,
he made terrible threats.
And I had no shelter in sleep by night or sleep by day:
Time stood like a deathmaster over me,
letting the minutes drop.
Now I am free!
Today I shake loose from my fear
of her, my fear of him.   1060
And to tell you the truth,
she did more damage.
She lived in my house
and drank
my lifeblood neat!
Now things are different.
She may go on making threats—but so what?
From now on, I pass my days in peace.

ELECTRA OIMOI TALAINA.
Now I have grief enough to cry out OIMOI—   1070
Orestes! Poor cold thing.
As you lie in death
your own mother insults you.
What a fine sight!

CLYTEMNESTRA Well you're no fine sight.
But he looks as fine as can be.

ELECTRA Nemesis! Hear her!

CLYTEMNESTRA Nemesis *has* heard me. And she has answered.

ELECTRA Batter away. This is your hour of luck.

CLYTEMNESTRA And you think you will stop me, you and Orestes?   1080

ELECTRA It is we who are stopped. There's no stopping you.

CLYTEMNESTRA Stranger, you deserve reward
if you really have put a stop on her traveling tongue.

OLD MAN Then I'll be on my way, if all is well.

CLYTEMNESTRA Certainly not! You've earned better
of me and the man who dispatched you.
No, you go inside.
Just leave her out here
to go on with her evil litany.

Exit CLYTEMNESTRA *and* OLD MAN *into house*

ELECTRA Well how did she look to you—shattered by grief?   1090
Heartbroken mother bewailing her only son?
No—you saw her—she went off laughing!
O TALAIN'EGO.
Orestes beloved,
as you die you destroy me.
You have torn away the part of my mind
where hope was—
my one hope in you
to live,
to come back,   1100
to avenge us.
Now where can I go?
Alone I am.
Bereft of you. Bereft of father.
Should I go back into slavery?
Back to those creatures who cut down my father?
What a fine picture.
No.
I will not go back inside that house.
No. At this door   1110
I will let myself lie
unloved.
I will wither my life.
If it aggravates them,

they can kill me.
Yes it will be a grace if I die.
To exist is pain.
Life is no desire of mine anymore.

CHORUS Where are you lightnings of Zeus!   *strophe 1*
       Where are you scorching Sun!   1120
       In these dark pits you leave us dark!

ELECTRA E E AIAI.

CHORUS Child, why do you cry?

ELECTRA PHEU.

CHORUS Don't make that sound.

ELECTRA You will break me.

CHORUS How?

ELECTRA If you bring me hope and I know he is dead,
        you will harm my heart.

CHORUS But think of Amphiaraus: *antistrophe 1*   1130
       he was a king once,
       snared by a woman in nets of gold.
       Now under the earth

ELECTRA E E IO.

CHORUS He is a king in the shadows of souls.

ELECTRA PHEU.

CHORUS Cry PHEU, yes! For his murderess—

ELECTRA was destroyed!

CHORUS Destroyed.

ELECTRA   I know—because an avenger arose.   1140
          I have no such person. That person is gone.

CHORUS   You are a woman marked for sorrow.   *strophe* 2

ELECTRA   Yes I know sorrow. Know it far too well.
          My life is a tunnel
          choked
          by the sweepings of dread.

CHORUS   We have watched you grieving.

ELECTRA   Then do not try—

CHORUS   What?

ELECTRA   To console me.   1150
          The fact is,
          there are no more hopes.
          No fine brothers.
          No comfort.

CHORUS   Death exists inside every mortal.   *antistrophe* 2

ELECTRA   Oh yes, but think of the hooves drumming down on him!
          See that thing
          dragging behind in the reins—

CHORUS   Too cruel.

ELECTRA   Yes. Death made him a stranger—   1160

CHORUS   PAPAI.

ELECTRA   Laid out
          somewhere
          not by my hands.
          Not with my tears.

                                        Enter CHRYSOTHEMIS

CHRYSOTHEMIS I am so happy, I ran here to tell you—
              putting good manners aside!
              I have good news for you that spells release
              from all your grieving.

ELECTRA Where could you find anything to touch my grief?   1170
         It has no cure.

CHRYSOTHEMIS Orestes is with us—yes! Know it from me—

              plain as you see me standing here!

ELECTRA You are mad.
         You are joking.

CHRYSOTHEMIS By the hearth of our father, this is no joke.
              He is with us. He is.

ELECTRA You poor girl.
         Who gave you this story?

CHRYSOTHEMIS No one gave me the story!   1180
              I saw the evidence with my own eyes.

ELECTRA What evidence?
         My poor girl, what has set you on fire?

CHRYSOTHEMIS Well listen, for gods' sake.
              Find out if I'm crazy or not.

ELECTRA All right, tell the tale, if it makes you happy.

CHRYSOTHEMIS Yes, I will tell all I saw.
              Well
              When I arrived at father's grave
              I saw milk dripping down from the top of the mound   1190
              and the tomb wreathed in flowers—
              flowers of every kind—what a shock!
              I peered all around—
              in case someone was sneaking up on me
              but no, the whole place was perfectly still.
              I crept near the tomb.

And there it was.
Right there on the edge.
A lock of hair, fresh cut.
As soon as I saw it, a bolt went through me —   1200
almost as if I saw his face,
I suddenly knew! Orestes.
Beloved Orestes.
I lifted it up. I said not a word.
I was weeping for joy.
And I know it now as I knew it then,
this offering had to come from him.
Who else would bother, except you or me?
And I didn't do it. I'm sure of that.
You couldn't do it — god knows you don't   1210
take a step from this house without getting in trouble.
And certainly mother has no such inclinations.

If she did, we would hear of it.
No, I tell you these offerings came from Orestes.
Oh Electra, lift your heart!
Bad luck can't last forever.
Long have we lived in shadows and shuddering:
today I think our future is opening out.

ELECTRA PHEU!
Poor lunatic. I feel sorry for you.   1220

CHRYSOTHEMIS What do you mean? Why aren't you happy?

ELECTRA You're dreaming, girl, lost in a moving dream.

CHRYSOTHEMIS Dreaming! How? I saw what I saw!

ELECTRA He is dead, my dear one.
He's not going to save you.
Dead, do you hear me? Dead. Forget him.

CHRYSOTHEMIS OIMOI TALAINA.
Who told you that?

ELECTRA Someone who was there when he died.

85

CHRYSOTHEMIS And where is this someone? It's all so strange.   1230

ELECTRA He's gone in the house. To entertain mother.

CHRYSOTHEMIS I don't want to hear this. I don't understand.
who put those offerings on father's tomb?

ELECTRA I think, most likely, someone who wished
to honor Orestes' memory.

CHRYSOTHEMIS What a fool I am—here I come racing for joy
to tell you my news, with no idea
how things really are.
The evils multiply.

ELECTRA Yes they do. But listen to me.   1240
You could ease our sorrow.

CHRYSOTHEMIS How? Raise the dead?

ELECTRA That's not what I meant. I am not quite insane.

CHRYSOTHEMIS Then what do you want? Am I capable of it?

ELECTRA All you need is the nerve—to do what I say.

CHRYSOTHEMIS If it benefits us, I will not refuse.

ELECTRA But you know nothing succeeds without work.

CHRYSOTHEMIS I do. I'll give you all the strength I have.

ELECTRA Good then, listen. Here is my plan.
You know, I think, our present contingent of allies: 1250
zero. Death took them.
We two are alone.
Up to now, while I heard that my brother was living
I cherished a hope
that he'd arrive one day to avenge his father.
But Orestes
no longer exists. I look to you.

You will not shrink back.
You will stand with your sister
and put to death the man who murdered your father: 1260
Aegisthus.
After all, what are you waiting for?
Let's be blunt, girl, what hope is left?
Your losses are mounting,
the property gone and
marriage
seems a fading dream at your age —
or do you still console yourself with thoughts of a
husband?
Forget it. Aegisthus is not so naive   1270
as to see children born from you or from me —
unambiguous grief for himself.
But now if you join in my plans,
you will win, in the first place,
profound and sacred respect from the dead below:
your father, your brother.
And second, people will call you noble.
That is your lineage, that is your future.
And besides, you will find a husband,
a good one: men like a woman with character.   1280
Oh don't you see? You'll make us famous!
People will cheer! They'll say
'Look at those two!' they'll say
'Look at the way they saved their father's house!
Against an enemy standing strong!
Risked their lives! Stood up to murder!
Those two deserve to be honored in public,
on every streetcorner and festival in the city —
there should be a prize for heroism like that!'
So they will speak of us.   1290
And whether we live or die doesn't matter:
that fame will stand.
Oh my dear one, listen to me.
Take on your father's work,
take up your brother's task,
make some refuge from evil for me
and for you.
Because you know,

there is a kind of excellence
in me and you—born in us—   1300
and it cannot live in shame.

CHORUS   In times like these, speaking or listening,
         forethought is your ally)

CHRYSOTHEMIS Well yes—and if this were a rational woman
             she would have stopped to think before she spoke.
             She is, unfortunately, mad.
             Tell me, what in the world do you have in mind
             as you throw on your armor
             and call me to your side?
             Look at yourself! You are female,   1310
             not male—born that way.
             And you're no match for them in strength or in luck.
             They are flush with fortune;
             our luck has trickled away.
             Really, Electra,
             who would think to topple a man of his stature?
             Who could ever get away with it?
             Be careful: this sort of blundering
             might make things worse for us—
             what if someone overhears!   1320
             And there is nothing whatever to win or to gain
             if we make ourselves famous and die in disgrace.
             Death itself is not the worst thing.
             Worse is to live
             when you want to die.
             So I beg you,
             before you destroy us
             and wipe out the family altogether,
             control your temper.
             As for your words,   1330
             I will keep them secret—for your sake.
             Oh Electra, get some sense! It is almost too late.
             Your strength is nothing,

             you cannot beat them: give up.

CHORUS Hear that? Foresight!—
no greater asset a person can have
than foresight combined with good sense.

ELECTRA Predictable.
I knew you'd say no.
Well: /   1340
alone then.
One hand will have to be enough.
One hand *is* enough.

Yes.

CHRYSOTHEMIS Too bad you weren't so resolved
on the day father died.
You could have finished the task.

ELECTRA Yes, I had the guts for it then, but no strategy.

CHRYSOTHEMIS Forget strategy—you'll live longer.

ELECTRA I gather you don't intend to help.   1350

CHRYSOTHEMIS Too risky for me.

ELECTRA You have your own strategy, I see.
I admire that.

But your cowardice appalls me.

CHRYSOTHEMIS One day you will say I was right.

ELECTRA Never.

CHRYSOTHEMIS The future will judge.

ELECTRA Oh go away. You give no help.

CHRYSOTHEMIS You take no advice.

ELECTRA Why not run off and tell all this to mother?   1360

CHRYSOTHEMIS I don't hate you that much.

ELECTRA At least realize you are driving me into dishonor.

CHRYSOTHEMIS Dishonor? No: foresight.

ELECTRA And I should conform to your version of justice?

CHRYSOTHEMIS When you are sane, you can think for us both.

ELECTRA Terrible to sound so right and be so wrong.

CHRYSOTHEMIS Well put! You describe yourself to a fault.

ELECTRA Do you deny that I speak for justice?

CHRYSOTHEMIS Let's just say there are times
when justice is too big a risk.   1370

ELECTRA I will not live by rules like those.

CHRYSOTHEMIS Go ahead then. You'll find out I was right.

ELECTRA I *do* go ahead. You can not deter me.

CHRYSOTHEMIS So you won't change your plan?

ELECTRA Immorality isn't a plan. It is the enemy.

CHRYSOTHEMIS You don't hear a single word I say.

ELECTRA Oh it was all decided long ago.

CHRYSOTHEMIS Well I'll be off.
It's clear you could never bring yourself
to praise my words, nor I your ways.   1380

ELECTRA Yes. You do that. You be off.
But I will not follow you,
no.
Never.
Not even if you beg me.

When
I look in your eyes I see emptiness.

CHRYSOTHEMIS If that is your attitude,
that is your attitude.
When you're in deep trouble,   1390
you'll say I was right.

Exit CHRYSOTHEMIS

CHORUS Why is it—   *strophe* 1
we look at birds in the air,
we see it makes sense
the way they care
for the life of those who sow and sustain them—
why
is it
we don't do the same?
No: 1400
by lightning of Zeus,
by Themis of heaven,
not long

free of pain!
O
sound going down
to the dead in the
ground,
take a voice,
take my voice,   1410
take down
pity
below
to Atreus' dead:
tell them shame.
Tell them there is no dancing.

Because   *antistrophe* 1
here is a house falling sick
falling now
between two children battling,   1420
and there is no more level of love in the days.

Betrayed,
alone
she goes down in the waves:
Electra,
grieving for death,
for her father,
as a nightingale
grieving always.
Nor   1430
does she think
to fear dying,
no!
she is glad
to go dark.
As a
killer
of furies,
as a pureblooded
child   1440
of the father who sowed her.
No one well-born   *strophe 2*
is willing to live

with evil,
with shame,
with a name made nameless.
O child,
child,
you made your life a wall of tears
against dishonor: 1450
you fought and you won.
For they call you
the child of his mind,

child of his excellence.
I pray you raise your hand   *antistrophe 2*
and crush the ones
who now
crush you!
For I see you subsisting
in mean part,   1460
and yet

you are one who kept faith
with the living laws,
kept faith
in the clear reverence
of Zeus.

Enter ORESTES *and servant with urn*

ORESTES Tell me ladies, did we get the right directions?
Are we on the right road? Is this the place?

CHORUS What place? What do you want?

ORESTES The place where Aegisthus lives.   1470

CHORUS Well here you are. Your directions were good.

ORESTES Which one of you, then, will tell those within?
Our arrival will please them.

CHORUS Her—as nearest of kin, she is the right one to
announce you.

ORESTES Please, my lady, go in and tell them
that certain Phocians are asking for Aegisthus.

ELECTRA OIMOI TALAIN'.
Oh no. Don't say that. Don't say you have come with
evidence of the stories we heard.   1480

ORESTES I don't know what you heard.
Old Strophius sent me with news of Orestes.

ELECTRA Oh stranger, what news? Fear comes walking into me.

ORESTES We have his remains in a small urn here—
for he's dead, as you see.

ELECTRA OI 'GO TALAINA.
Oh no. No. Not this thing in your hands.
No.

ORESTES If you have tears to shed for Orestes,
         this urn is all that holds his body now.   1490

ELECTRA Oh stranger, allow me, in god's name—
         if this vessel does really contain him,
         to hold it in my hands.
         For myself, for the whole generation of us,
         I have tears to keep,
         I have ashes to weep.

ORESTES (to servant with urn): Bring it here, give it to her, whoever
         she is.
         It is no enemy asking this.
         She is someone who loved him,
         or one of his blood.   1500

ELECTRA If this were all you were, Orestes,
         how could your memory
         fill my memory,
         how is it your soul fills my soul?
         I sent you out, I get you back:
         tell me
         how could the difference be simply
         nothing?
         Look!
         You are nothing at all.   1510
         Just a crack where the light slipped through.
         Oh my child,
         I thought I could save you.
         I thought I could send you beyond.
         But there is no beyond.
         You might as well have stayed that day
         to share your father's tomb.
         Instead, somewhere, I don't know where—
         suddenly alone you stopped—
         where death was.   1520
         You stopped.
         And I would have waited
         and washed you
         and lifted you
         up from the fire,
         like a whitened coal.

Strangers are so careless!
Look how you got smaller, coming back.
OIMOI TALAINA.
All my love   1530
gone for nothing.
Days of my love, years of my love.
Into your child's fingers I put the earth and the sky.
No mother did that for you.
No nurse.
No slave.
I. Your sister
without letting go,
day after day, year after year,
and you my own sweet child.   1540

But death was a wind too strong for that.

One day three people vanished.
Father. You. Me. Gone.
Now our enemies rock with laughter.
And she runs mad for joy—
that creature
in the shape of your mother—
how often you said you would come
one secret evening and cut her throat!
But our luck cancelled that,   1550
whatever luck is.
And instead my beloved,
luck sent you back to me
colder than ashes,
later than shadow.
OIMOI MOI.
Pity,
PHEU PHEU
oh beloved,
OIMOI MOI   .   1560
as you vanish down that road.
Oh my love
take me there.
Let me dwell where you are.
I am already nothing.
I am already burning.

Oh my love, I was once part of you—
take me too!
Only void is between us.
And I see that the dead feel no pain.   1570

CHORUS Electra, be reasonable.
Your father was a mortal human being.
Orestes too—we all pay the same price for that.
Control yourself.

ORESTES PHEU PHEU.
What should I say? This is
impossible! I cannot hold my tongue much longer.

ELECTRA What is the matter? What are you trying to say?

ORESTES Is this the brilliant Electra?

ELECTRA This is Electra. Brilliant no more.   1580

ORESTES OIMOI TALAINES.
It hurts me to look at you.

ELECTRA Surely, stranger, you're not feeling sorry for me?

ORESTES It shocks me, the way you look: do they abuse you?

ELECTRA Yes, in fact. But who are you?

ORESTES PHEU
What an ugly, loveless life for a girl.

ELECTRA Why do you stare at me? Why are you so sympathetic?

ORESTES I had no idea how bad my situation really is.

ELECTRA And what makes you realize that? Something I said?

ORESTES Just to see the outline of your suffering.   1590

ELECTRA Yet this is only a fraction of it you see.

ORESTES What could be worse than this?

ELECTRA To live in the same house with killers.

ORESTES What killers? What evil are you hinting at?

ELECTRA My own father's killers.
         And I serve them as a slave. By compulsion.

ORESTES Who compels you?

ELECTRA Mother she is called. Mother she is not.

ORESTES How do you mean? Does she strike you? Insult you?

ELECTRA Yes. And worse.   1600

ORESTES But have you no one to protect you?
         No one to stand in her way?

ELECTRA No. There was someone. Here are his ashes.

ORESTES Oh girl. How I pity the dark life you live.

ELECTRA No one else has ever pitied me, you know.

ORESTES No one else has ever been part of your grief.

ELECTRA Do you mean you are somehow part of my family?

ORESTES I'll explain—if these women are trustworthy.

ELECTRA Oh yes, you can trust them. Speak freely.

ORESTES Give back the urn, then, and you will hear everything.   1610

ELECTRA No! Don't take this from me, for god's sake,
         whoever you are!

ORESTES Come now, do as I say. It is the right thing.

ELECTRA No! In all reverence no please—don't take this away.
It is all that I love.

ORESTES I forbid you to keep it.

ELECTRA O TALAIN'EGO SETHEN.
Orestes! What if
they take from me
even the rites of your death!   1620

ORESTES Hush, now. That language is wrong.

ELECTRA Wrong to mourn my own dead brother?

ORESTES Wrong for you to say that word.

ELECTRA How did I lose the right to call him brother?

ORESTES Your rights you have. Your brother you don't.

ELECTRA Do I not stand here with Orestes himself in my hands?

ORESTES No, in fact. That Orestes is a lie.

ELECTRA Then where in the world is the poor boy's grave?

ORESTES Nowhere. The living need no grave.

ELECTRA Child, what are you saying?   1630

ORESTES Nothing but the truth.

ELECTRA The man is alive?

ORESTES As I live and breathe.

ELECTRA You—?

ORESTES Look at this ring—our father's—

ELECTRA Father's!

ORESTES —and see what I mean.

ELECTRA Oh love, you break on me like light!

ORESTES Yes like light!

ELECTRA Oh voice, have you come out of nowhere?   1640

ORESTES Nowhere but where you are.

ELECTRA Do I hold you now in my hands?

ORESTES Now and forever.

ELECTRA Ladies, my friends, my people, look!
        Here stands Orestes:
        dead by device
        now by device brought back to life!

ORESTES I see, child. And at this reversal,
        my tears are falling for joy.

ELECTRA IO GONAI.   *strophe*   1650
        You exist!
        You came back,
        you found me—

ORESTES Yes, I am here. Now keep silent a while.

ELECTRA Why?

ORESTES Silence is better. Someone inside might overhear.

ELECTRA By Artemis unbroken! I would not
        dignify with fear
        the dull surplus of females
        who huddle in that house!   1660

ORESTES Careful! There is war in women too,
        as you know by experience, I think.

99

ELECTRA OTOTOTOTOI TOTOI.
You drive me back down my desperation—
that unclouded

incurable
never forgotten
evil
growing inside my life.

ORESTES I know, but we should talk of those deeds   1670
when the moment is right.

ELECTRA Every arriving moment of my life   *antistrophe*
has a right
to tell those deeds!
And this chance to speak freely is hard won.

ORESTES Precisely. Safeguard it.

ELECTRA How?

ORESTES When the time is unsuitable, no long speeches.

ELECTRA But how could silence be the right way to greet
you—simply   1680
coming
out of nowhere
like a miracle?

ORESTES It was a miracle set in motion by the gods.

ELECTRA Ah.

That is a vast claim
and much more beautiful,
to think
some god
has brought you here.   1690
Some god: yes! That must be true.

ORESTES Electra, I do not like to curb your rejoicing
but I am afraid when you lose control.

ELECTRA Oh but my love—
       now that you have travelled back down all those years

       to meet my heart,
       over all this grief of mine,
       do not
       oh love—

ORESTES What are you asking?   1700

ELECTRA Do not turn your face from me.
       Don't take yourself away.

ORESTES Of course not. No one else will take me either.

ELECTRA Do you mean that?

ORESTES Yes I do.

ELECTRA Oh beloved,
       I heard your voice
       when I had no hope
       and my heart leapt away from me
       calling   1710
       you.
       I was in sorrow.
       But now
       I am holding you,
       now you are visible—
       light of the face I could never forget.

ORESTES Spare me these words.
       You don't need to teach me my mother is evil
       or how Aegisthus drains the family wealth,
       pours it out like water,   1720
       sows it to the wind.
       We've no time for all that—talk is expensive.
       What I need now are the practical details:
       where we should hide, where we can leap out
       and push that enemy laughter
       right back down their throats!

But be careful she doesn't read
the fact of our presence
straight from the glow on your face.
You must keep on lamenting   1730
my fictitious death.
Time enough
for lyres and laughter
when we've won the day.

ELECTRA Your will and my will are one: identical, brother.
For I take all my joy from you,
none is my own.
Nor could I harm you ever so slightly
at any price: it would be a disservice
to the god who stands beside us now.   1740
So. You know what comes next.
Aegisthus has gone out,
mother is home.
And don't worry:
she'll see no glow on my face.
Hatred put out the light in me a long time ago.
Besides, since I saw you
my tears keep running down—
tears, joy, tears all mixed up together.
How could I stop?   1750
I saw you come down that road a dead man,
I looked again and saw you alive.
You have used me strangely.
Why—if father suddenly came back to life
I wouldn't call it fantastic.

Believe what you see.
But
now you have come,
I am yours to command.
Alone,   1760
I would have done one of two things:
deliver myself or else die.

ORESTES Quiet! I hear someone coming out.

ELECTRA Go inside, strangers.
         You are bringing a gift
         they can neither reject nor rejoice in.

                                        Enter OLD MAN

OLD MAN Idiots! Have you lost your wits completely,
         and your instinct to survive as well—
         or were you born brainless?
         You're not on the brink of disaster now,   1770
         you're right in the eye of it, don't you see that?
         Why, except for me standing guard at the door here
         this long while, your plans
         would have been in the house
         before yourselves!
         Good thing I took caution.
         Now cut short the speechmaking,
         stifle your joy
         and go in the house. Go!
         Delay is disaster in things like this.   1780
         Get it over with: that's the point now.

ORESTES How will I find things inside?

OLD MAN Perfect. No one will know you.

ORESTES You reported me dead?

OLD MAN You are deep in hell, so far as they know.

ORESTES Are they happy at this?

OLD MAN I'll tell you that later. For now,
         the whole plan is unfolding beautifully.
         Even the ugly parts.

ELECTRA Who is this man, brother?   1790

ORESTES Don't you know him?

ELECTRA Not even remotely.

ORESTES You don't know the man into whose hands you put me,
         once long ago?

ELECTRA What man? What are you saying?

ORESTES The man who smuggled me off to Phocia,
         thanks to your foresight.

ELECTRA Him? Can it be? That man was
         the one trustworthy soul I could find in the house,
         the day father died!   1800

ORESTES That's who he is. Do not question me further.

ELECTRA *(to the* OLD MAN*)* I bless you like the light of day!
         I bless you
         as the savior of the house of Agamemnon!
         How did you come? Is it really you—
         who pulled us up from the pit that day?
         I bless your hands,
         I bless your feet,
         I bless the sweet roads you walked!
         How strange   1810
         you were beside me all that time and gave no sign.
         Strange—to destroy me with lies
         when you had such sweet truth to tell.
         Bless you, father!—Yes, father.
         That is who I see when I look at you now.

         There is no man on earth I have hated and loved like
                 you
         on the one same day.

OLD MAN Enough, now. As for all the stories in between—
         there will be nights and days
         to unravel them, Electra.   1820
         But for you two, standing here,
         I have just one word: act!
         Now is the moment!
         Now Clytemnestra is alone.
         Now there is not one man in the house.

If you wait you will have to fight others,
more skilled and more numerous. Think!

ORESTES Well, Pylades, no more speeches.
As quick as we can
into the house—after   1830
we pay our respects
to the gods of this doorway.

Exit ORESTES *and* PYLADES *followed by the* OLD MAN

ELECTRA King Apollo! Graciously hear them.
Hear me too! I have been devout,
I have come to you often,

bringing you gifts of whatever I had.
Now again I come with all that I have:
Apollo wolfkiller! I beg you!
I call out—
I fall to my knees!   1840
please send your mind over us,
inform our strategies,
show
how the gods reward
unholy action!

CHORUS Look where he comes grazing forward,   *strophe*
blood bubbling over his lips: Ares!
As a horizontal scream into the house
go the hunters of evil,
the raw and deadly dogs.   1850
Not long now:
the blazing dream of my head is crawling out.

Here he comes like a stealing shadow,   *antistrophe*
like a footprint of death into the rooms,
stalking the past

with freshcut blood in his hands.
It is Hermes who guides him
down a blindfold of shadow—
straight to the finish line: not long now!

ELECTRA   My ladies! The men   1860
          are about to accomplish the deed—
          be silent and wait.

CHORUS   How? What are they doing?

ELECTRA   She is dressing the urn. They are standing beside her.

CHORUS   But why did you come running out here?

ELECTRA   To watch that Aegisthus doesn't surprise us.

CLYTEMNESTRA   (*within*) AIAI IO.
               Rooms
               filled with murder!

ELECTRA   Someone inside screams—do you hear?   1870

CHORUS   Yes I hear. It makes my skin crawl.

CLYTEMNESTRA   OIMOI TALAIN'.
               Aegisthus, where are you?

ELECTRA   There! Again! Someone calls out.

CLYTEMNESTRA   Oh child my child, pity the mother who bore you!

ELECTRA   Yet you had little enough pity for him
          and none for his father!

CHORUS   Alas for the city.
          Alas for a whole race thrown and shattered:
          the shape that followed you down the days   1880
          is dying now, dying away.

CLYTEMNESTRA   OMOI.
               I am hit!

ELECTRA   Hit her a second time, if you have the strength!

CLYTEMNESTRA   OMOI MAL' AUTHIS.
               Again!

ELECTRA If only Aegisthus could share this!

CHORUS The curses are working.
Under the ground
dead men are alive   1890
with their black lips moving,
black mouths sucking
on the soles of killer' feet.

Here they come,
hands soaked with red: Ares is happy!
Enough said.

ELECTRA Orestes, how does it go?

ORESTES Good, so far—at least so far as Apollo's oracle was
good.

ELECTRA Is the creature dead?   1900

ORESTES Your good mother will not insult you anymore.

CHORUS Stop! I see Aegisthus coming yes, it is him.

ELECTRA Children, get back!

ORESTES Where do you see him—

ELECTRA There—marching right down on us
full of joy.

CHORUS Go quick to the place just inside the front door.
You have won the first round. Now for the second.

ORESTES Don't worry. We will finish this.

ELECTRA Hurry. Go to it.   1910

ORESTES Yes I am gone.

ELECTRA And leave this part to me.

CHORUS Why not drop a few friendly words in his ear—
        so his moment of justice may come
        as a surprise.

                                        Enter AEGISTHUS

AEGISTHUS Does anyone know where those Phoeian strangers are?
           People say they have news of Orestes
           dead in a chariot crash.
           You!
           yes you!—you've never been shy   1920
           to speak your mind.
           And obviously this matter most concerns you.

ELECTRA Yes of course I know, for I do keep track
         of the fortunes of the family.

AEGISTHUS Where are they then,
           the strangers?—tell me.

ELECTRA Inside the house, for they've fallen upon
         the perfect hostess.

AEGISTHUS And it's true they bring a report of his death?

ELECTRA No—better: they have evidence,   1930
         not just words.

AEGISTHUS We can see proof?

ELECTRA You can, indeed, though it's no pretty sight.

AEGISTHUS Well this is good news. Unusual, coming from you.

ELECTRA Relish it while you can.

AEGISTHUS Silence! I say throw open the gates!
           for every Mycenaean and Argive to see—
           in case you had placed empty hopes
           in this man—
           take my bit on your tongue   1940
           or learn the hard way.

ELECTRA As for me, I am playing my part to the end.
I've learned to side with the winners.

A shrouded corpse is disclosed with ORESTES *and* PYLADES
standing beside it.

AEGISTHUS O Zeus! I see here a man fallen by the jealousy of god
—but
if that remark offends,
I unsay it.

Uncover the eyes. Uncover it all.
I should pay my respects.

ORESTES Uncover it yourself.   1950
This isn't my corpse—it's yours.
Yours to look at, yours to eulogize.

AEGISTHUS Yes good point. I have to agree.
You there—Clytemnestra must be about in the house—
call her for me.

ORESTES She is right here before you. No need to look elsewhere.

AEGISTHUS OIMOI.
What do I see!

ORESTES You don't know the face?

AEGISTHUS Caught! But *who set the trap?*   1960

ORESTES Don't you realize yet
that you're talking to dead men alive?

AEGISTHUS OIMOI.
I do understand. You are Orestes.

ORESTES At last.

AEGISTHUS I'm a dead man. No way out.
But let me just say—

ELECTRA No!
Don't let him speak—
by the gods! Brother—no speechmaking now!   1970
When a human being is so steeped in evil as this one
what is gained by delaying his death?
Kill him at once.
Throw his corpse out
for scavengers to get.
Nothing less than this
can cut the knot of evils
inside me.

ORESTES Get in with you, quickly.
This is no word game: 1980
your life is at stake.

AEGISTHUS Why take me inside?
If the deed is honorable, what need of darkness?
You aren't ready to kill?

ORESTES Don't give me instructions, just get yourself in:
You will die on the spot
where you slaughtered my father.

AEGISTHUS Must these rooms see
the whole evil of Pelops' race,
present and future?   1990

ORESTES They will see yours, I can prophesy.

AEGISTHUS That is no skill you got from your father!

ORESTES Your answers are quick, your progress slow.
Go.

AEGISTHUS You lead the way.

ORESTES No you go first.

AEGISTHUS Afraid I'll escape?

ORESTES You shall not die on your own terms.
I will make it bitter for you.
And let such judgment fall   2000
on any who wish to break the law:
kill them!
The evil were less.

Exit ORESTES *and* AEGISTHUS, *followed by* ELECTRA, *into*
the house

CHORUS O seed of Atreus:
you suffered and broke free,

you took aim and struck;
you have won your way through
to the finish.

Exit CHORUS

NOTES ON THE TEXT

A few formal terms: The basic divisions of a Greek tragedy, according to the tradition, is into prologue, parodos, episodes, and stasima.
A Greek tragedy contains a variety of levels of speech, in the most
general terms the meter of spoken verse (iambic trimeters) and lyric.
The prologue and the episodes are usually in iambic trimeter. Characters may speak to each other or to the chorus. A lyric exchange between the chorus and one or more characters is a *kommos*. The *parodos* is the entry song of the chorus (in the *Electra* this takes the form
of a *kommos* between Electra and the chorus). A *stasimon* is a choral
song that divides two *episodes*. The *episodes*, which are mostly in iambic trimeter, are what we would call scenes; the final *episode*, which
ends the drama, can also be called the *exodos*. These choral songs are
typically constructed of strophe, antistrophe, and epode. A strophe
is a stanza, while an antistrophe is a stanza whose metrical form
closely follows that of a strophe. An epode is a single stanza which follows a paired strophe and antistrophe, but whose metrical form is
unique.

1–162 This prologue has two parts, a dialogue in iambics spoken by Orestes and the
Old Man and a monody by Electra. The Old Man is called Paedagogus
here because he is the servant who raised Orestes

*The scene: the door to the palace is in the background, and beside it stands a statue
of Apollo.* ORESTES *and* PYLADES *are distinguished from the* OLD MAN *by their dress,
since he is a servant.* ORESTES *and* PYLADES *are dressed as young men of nobility and
are wearing travelers' hats.*

6 *The grove of Io.* . . . This may not be a specific place, but rather it may refer to all of Argos. There are parallels between Orestes' story and that of Io, which is given in the Glossary.

7–9 . . . *the marketplace / named for Apollo, / wolfkiller god.* This Argive feature is not identified. See the Glossary for "Apollo wolfkiller."

10 . . . *the famous temple of Hera.* The Argive temple to Hera is approximately a mile south of Mycenae.

17 *From the hands of your sister.* Neither Aeschylus nor Euripides say that Electra saved Orestes, and this is probably the invention of Sophocles.

107 *IO MOI MOI DYSTENOS.* This is a traditional cry of grief. '*Dystenos*' means wretched. Inarticulate or nearly inarticulate cries of grief, pain, sorrow, surprise, etc., are common in this play. See the Translator's Preface.

115–62 Monody (sung verse); the meter changes in the Greek text from iambic trimeter to a lyric meter, in this case lyric anapests.

144 *nightingale.* See Philomela in the Glossary.

163–333 The parodos consists of a duet (*kommos*) between the chorus and Electra.

199 *the bird who calls Itys!* Philomela again, here linked to Niobe (see Glossary).

282 *pain on pain to pay* This repeats the alliteration of *p* in the Greek line: *poinima pathea pathein poroi.*

334–647 In the first episode, Electra begins with a monologue, and the rest of the scene is a dialogue between Electra and Chrysothemis.

338 *I am ashamed* . . . In the Greek text, Electra's first word is "I am ashamed." Perhaps there is a hint here that Electra is the opposite of Clytemnestra, who said "I am not ashamed" at the beginning of two major speeches in Aeschylus' *Agamemnon* (856 and 1373).

444 Enter Chrysothemis As we will soon hear, Chrysothemis is more richly dressed than Electra, who is herself probably dressed as a servant. There is no embroidery on Electra's "belt," and thus we can assume that such embroidery is visible on Chrysothemis' costume as it is on that of Clytemnestra. As a noble woman, Chrysothemis probably should

have an attendant, but she carries at least some of the offerings in her
own hands.

466 *not a word is your own.* . . . Kells claims this charge is not fair, but it seems
accurate to me. Chrysothemis is not simply in the wrong. By accepting
the benefits of a corrupt government, she shares responsibility for its
acts to some degree.

468 *sensible* This term (*phronein*) is prominent here, just as it was in the dialogue
of Antigone and Ismene in Sophocles' *Antigone*. It can apply both to
"justice" and to "expediency." Electra ironically uses the word in its
expediency signification. Chrysothemis later ends her speech with this
word ("sensible," 530).

543 *we have masters, we must bend* This is the language of "expediency." Electra
counters with "lick their boots"—that is, Chrysothemis' position is one
of base flattery (*thopeia*). Chrysothemis counters with a charge of stupidity (*aboulia*, 546). Prometheus uses similar language in a similar
situation in Aeschylus' *Prometheus Bound*. He sneeringly urges the chorus to "flatter" Zeus (*thopte*, 937). Hermes urges him to "think straight"
(*eu phronein*, 1000). He accuses Prometheus of preferring audacity to
"good thought" (*euboulia*, 1035)

586 *plain stupidity.* Chrysothemis ends her account of the dream and returns to her
earlier remarks, repeating the word *stupidity* (*aboulia*) (see preceeding
note).

648–91 In the first stasimon, the chorus reflect on Clytemnestra's dream: justice will
come.

663–69 *Vengeance . . . where marriage should never have happened!* The Greek word
for vengeance is *Erinys* (a Fury). Once again, the chorus uses archaic
language. In the very difficult Greek of this passage, the marriage of
Clytemnestra and Aegisthus is said to be "without a bed, without a
bride" (*alektra, anumpha*). The pun on Electra's name is probably
intentional. The same pun appears in 1266–67 when Electra tells Chrysothemis that she will grow old "unbedded" (*alektra*) if Aegisthus and
Clytemnestra remain in power. Thus the actions of Clytemnestra and
Aegisthus have made their own marriage dysfunctional (i.e., their children have no inheritance rights, no status) and made marriage impossible for everyone else in the royal line. Electra herself is only one
embodiment of that frustration.

692–1391 The second episode begins with the entry of Clytemnestra, and the first part of the episode is a dialogue with Electra. The Old Man then enters and gives his messenger speech, followed by comments by all three actors, after which Clytemnestra and the Old Man exit. Electra remains and sings a *kommos* with the chorus. Chrysothemis enters; the sisters quarrel; Chrysothemis exits.

745 ... *about the dead man and my sister as well* We need only examine the speech that follows to see that this is not spoken in complete candor. Electra is an artful rhetorician as well as a passionate one.

755–67 *Ask Artemis ... Hence, the sacrifice.* Aeschylus does not give a specific human action as the cause of Artemis' wrath at Aulis. Rather, the seer Calchas infers that wrath from an omen. Euripides more or less follows the version given here. These events are the subject of Euripides' *Iphigenia in Aulis*.

788 *You share ... making children.* The Greek has a wonderful run of *p*'s here: "**pa**lamnaioi, meth hou / **pa**tera ton amon **pros**then exa**po**lesas, / kai **pai**dopoieis." Electra is literally spewing. The children of Clytemnestra and Aegisthus were Aletes and Erigone. There are references to plays by Sophocles with each of these names. (See Hyginus, *Fabula* 122 for stories about these children and Electra and Orestes.)

816 *bitch* This word is not found in the Greek text, and there seems to be no hint here (as there is elsewhere) that Electra is a "dog" and hence a Fury. Rather, this translation refers to the Greek word *shameless*, also a quality associated with dogs.

946–56 *Achaea ... Boeotian* The competitors seem to be diverse in geography and in chronology. One is from Achaea, on the north coast of the Peloponnese, one is a Spartan from the central Peloponnese, two are from Libya (and thus strictly speaking postheroic); one is from Thessaly in north eastern Greece, one is Aetolian, from west of Delphi, one is a Magnesian and one is an Aenian—both tribes in Thessaly mentioned in Homer; and one is a Boeotian and one is an Athenian.

990 *He had put his faith in the finish.* There may be some allegorical point in this detail. In Book 10 of the *Republic*, Plato has Socrates defend just action by saying that the just man finishes the race, while the unjust man is tripped up. Here Orestes does not seem to finish the race, but of course he will in fact do so.

1077 *Nemesis! Hear her!* Electra appeals to the goddess of retribution to punish Clytemnestra for saying that her son Orestes is "well off" being dead. Clytemnestra's reply probably refers to Orestes' death threats against her, for which Nemesis has punished him.

1092 *She went off laughing . . .* Here as often in Greek literature and in Sophocles, a person wronged imagines his or her enemies laughing.

1125 *Don't make that sound.* There is a very interesting scholium (an ancient or medieval note preserved in our manuscript tradition) on this line: "It is necessary for the actor to look up to heaven as he makes this cry and to hold out his hands. The chorus restrains him by saying 'Do not say anything excessive.'"

1203 *Beloved Orestes.* In a play full of expressions of love, this is the most extreme: "most beloved of all mortals."

1204 *I said not a word.* Literally, "I did not utter a word of ill omen." Jebb assumes she refrained from reproaching Orestes for coming too late. He rejects the view that a cry of joy would be ill-omened at her father's tomb. I believe the remote model here is Odysseus' remark to the old maid after she sees the suitors have been killed in the *Odyssey* (quoted in the introduction, p. 34). What Chrysothemis refrains from doing is letting out a shout of celebration.

1246 *if it benefits . . .* Chrysothemis' use of "benefit" (*opheleia*) marks this as an expediency position.

1266–67 *marriage / seems a fading dream at your age.* Electra says that *Chrysothemis* will be unbedded (*alektra*)! See the note on lines 663–69.

1275 *profound and sacred respect . . .* Chrysothemis will get the reverence (*eusebeia*) of the dead. One of Electra's key words.

1277 *noble.* The Greek word here is *eleuthera* (free). Chrysothemis claimed earlier (460) that she was free. Electra has at this point stripped away all of Chrysothemis' rationalizations.

1303 *forethought (prometheia)* The chorus points out to the glaring deficiency of this speech. What Electra proposes defies probability. Thus they prepare us for Chrysothemis' speech.

1304–5 *and if this were a rational woman / she would have stopped to think before she spoke.* Chrysothemis immediately uses two key words to a person of her character, "rational" (literally "wits" [*phrenon*]) and "stopped to think" (literally "caution," [*eulabeia*]).

1334 *you cannot beat them: give up.* Electra ended her speech with a heroic slogan: the noble prefer death to shameful life. Chrysothemis answers with one from the world of politics: the weaker must yield to the stronger.

1335 *Foresight!* (*pronoia*) The chorus has the values of any group and thus it places success above all. They cannot help but be alienated by Electra's disregard of good sense. The result, dramatically, is to leave Electra isolated at this point. She persists.

1342 *One hand will have to be enough.* A more literal translation is "the deed is to be done" (*drasteon*). The use of the verbal adjective is typical of Sophoclean heroes.

1392–1466 The Second stasimon consists of the chorus' praise of Electra.

1436–8 *as a / killer / of furies . . .* The twin furies are Aegisthus and Clytemnestra, so called because of the ruin they have caused.

1437–41 *as a pure-blooded / child / of the father . . .* The word "of good father" (*eupatris*) is closely related to "born of good fathers" (*eupatrides*), a term used of the Athenian aristocracy. Electra of course is literally "of a good father" for by her behavior she ratifies his virtue.

1467–1830 In the third episode, Orestes enters, Electra laments over the urn, and Orestes reveals himself. Electra and Orestes sing a duet. The Old Man enters, and the three characters speak, after which Orestes and the Old Man exit into the palace. Electra gives a short prayer and follows.

1482 *Old Strophius sent me with news of Orestes.* Orestes seems to get the names wrong. Phanoteus is the one who is supposed to be sending the body to Argos. Although it is not mentioned in this play, elsewhere Strophius is said to be Orestes' ally and the father of Pylades. His error passes without being noticed. Perhaps it is a sign of his nervousness.

1614 *No! in all reverence . . .* Literally, "not by your chin," a traditional gesture of appeal. It is a stage direction. Electra holds the urn in one hand; she appeals to Orestes with the other.

1651 *You exist!* Electra shifts into lyrics at this point, but Orestes speaks in iambic trimeter. Her joy knows no bounds, and Orestes keeps reminding her that there are bounds.

1846–59 This short song of the chorus is the third stasimon. They use traditional language to describe what has happened. The stage is momentarily empty—an unusual event in Greek tragedy.

1850 *the raw and deadly dogs . . .* These are the Furies. The language is traditional.

1856 *with freshcut blood in his hands.* An exact translation of this startling line.

1860–2008 In the final episode, or exodos, Electra enters, and in a short *kommos* three excited actions occur: Electra and the chorus respond to Clytemnestra's off-stage cries; Electra queries Orestes after he leaves the palace; the chorus see Aegisthus coming and Orestes reenters the palace to await him. Aegisthus enters (the meter reverts to iambics) and speaks to Electra. Electra opens the door, and Orestes and Pylades exit from the palace with a covered corpse. Aegisthus, Orestes, and Electra speak. Aegisthus enters the building, forced inside by Orestes. Choral comment.

GLOSSARY

ACHAEANS: Homer refers to the Greeks as Achaeans or Dorians or Argives. Greeks refer to themselves as Hellenes. "Greek" is the name used for them by the Romans.

ACHAEA: In historical times, Achaea was the name of a region located on the southern coast of the Bay of Corinth.

ACHERON: a river in the underworld.

AEGISTHUS: Aegisthus is the son of Thyestes. In revenge for a wrong, Atreus murdered the children of his brother Thyestes and after feeding them to him revealed what he had done. Aegisthus escaped the fate of his brothers and grew up to avenge this crime by killing the son of Atreus, Agamemnon. In Aeschylus' play, *Agamemnon*, Aegisthus tells this story and claims that his cause is just.

AENIAN: The Aenians are a tribe mentioned in the *Iliad* as one of the contingents on the Greek (i.e., Achaean) side (2.749). Although they were involved in hostilities against the Spartans in 420 B.C., they are probably here for the epic reminiscence.

AETOLIAN: Aetolia lies along the north shore of the Bay of Corinth, to the west of Delphi.

AGAMEMNON: leader of the Achaean armies in the *Iliad*. In the *Odyssey* (Book 11, lines 404–34), set in Hades, he tells of his murder by his wife and Aegisthus on his return. Agamemnon and his brother Menelaus are the sons of Atreus.

AMPHIARAUS: one of the seven who fought and were defeated at Thebes, in support of Polynices' claim on the Theban throne. Polynices bribed Amphiaraus' wife Eriphyle to force her husband to go, and he went knowing that he would die at Thebes. In the battle, the earth opened and he vanished into the ground. He had more than one mantic shrine in Greece in historical times. The champion who avenged him was Alcmaeon, who killed his mother.

APOLLO: This Greek god has his main temple and oracle at Delphi, where games were held in his honor. The well-known statue usually called the "Charioteer of Delphi," which was created about fifty years before this play was produced, gives us an idea of how the audience of this play would have pictured a driver in the chariot race at Delphi in which Orestes is said to have been killed. Apollo's oracle was often consulted by Greeks. His responses were often of a puzzling nature. Apollo's insistence that Orestes kill his father's murderers "with a trick" is found in all versions of this story in tragedy.

APOLLO WOLFKILLER: "Lykaios," a regular epithet or cult name of Apollo, can be derived from *lykos,* the Greek word for wolf. The Old Man points out that the marketplace is named for Apollo wolfkiller (7–8), and Clytemnestra and Electra both pray to Apollo as "wolfkiller Apollo." In Clytemnestra's speech (870) this phrase is simply translated "Lycian Apollo."

ARES: the god of war. His name often stands for violence of any sort.

ARGOS, ARGIVE: "Argive" is one of the names used for the Greeks by Homer. In this play, "Argos" and "Argive" refer to the region in which Mycenae is located.

ARTEMIS: goddess associated with animals and the hunt, sister of Apollo. She is called "unbroken" because of her virginity and independence. Women called on Artemis in childbirth. She hunted with her followers in the wild, and Agamemnon's boast was said by some Greek sources to have been that Artemis could not have made such a shot.

ATHENS: The only reference to Athens in this play comes in the report that the chariot from Athens won the race in which Orestes was said to have been killed. In Aeschylus, and in other versions, Orestes eventually stands trial for these murders in Athens.

ATREUS: the father of Agamemnon and Menelaus, who are called "Atreidai" or "sons of Atreus" in Homer and elsewhere.

AULIS: Before sailing to Troy, the Greek fleet assembled at Aulis, a place on the east coast of mainland Greece and site of a temple of Artemis.

BARCAEAN: Barca is a city in Cyrenaica in Libya. This is one of the two "Libyan" teams.

BOEOTIAN: Boeotia is a large plain north of Athens and east of Delphi.

CHRYSOTHEMIS: Chrysothemis is said to be a daughter of Agamemnon, along with Laodike and Iphianassa, in the *Iliad*, 9.144–47.

CLYTEMNESTRA: Clytemnestra, sister of Helen, is mentioned by Agamemnon in the *Iliad*, where he says that he cares for a concubine more than he does for her. Although his remarks occur in a bargaining context, they may hint at his later career. In the *Odyssey*, Agamemnon's ghost has much to say about her acts and how they reflect on women in general. She is the dominant character in Aeschylus' *Agamemnon* and plays a major role in Euripides' *Electra* and his *Iphigenia in Aulis*.

CRISA: a town near Delphi. The hippodrome at Delphi is located below the sanctuary in more level ground. This region is known as the plain of Crisa.

DELPHI: the mountain sanctuary of Apollo, where his main temple and oracle are located. Games were held here, which were one of the major athletic festivals in Greece. The oracle was consulted even in the fifth century. In the Greek historian Thucydides, a small Greek town asks the oracle how to end its civil war. Socrates says in the *Apology* that a friend of his went to Delphi and asked Apollo if Socrates was the wisest of men.

ERINYS OR FURY: The Greek word for Fury is Erinys (the plural is Erinyes). These goddesses are depicted in Aeschylus, where they make up the chorus of the *Eumenides*, the third play of the *Oresteia*, as terrible looking women with snakes in their hair. They prosecute Orestes before an Athenian court on the charge of matricide. In this play, there are several hints that Electra and Orestes represent the Furies of the traditional story in some sense. When Clytemnestra says that Electra "drinks her blood," that Electra is something like a fury is clear enough. The chorus describe Orestes and Pylades as "dogs" as they enter the house, and this is close to the concept of them in the *Oresteia*.

HADES: the lord of the land of the dead and husband of Persephone.

HERA: wife of Zeus and queen of the Olympian gods. Hera in the *Iliad* is a strong supporter of the Argives, and her sanctuary not far from Mycenae was a major shrine in historical times.

HERMES: god who guides the souls of the dead to Hades, but in this story he guides the avengers of the dead. He is also a great trickster and a good friend of his half-brother Apollo.

IO: the daughter of the river Inachos and the ancestor of the royal line at Argos. Aeschylus tells her story in his plays, *Suppliants* and *Prometheus Bound*. Zeus conceived a desire for Io, and due to Hera's hatred she was turned into a cow, guarded by Argus, a creature with a hundred eyes. After Hermes had killed Argus, a gadfly drove Io around the eastern Mediterranean to Egypt, where she regained her human form and produced a child, Epaphus, whose descendents eventually returned to Argos and produced the line of Argive kings that included Perseus and Heracles.

IPHIANASSA: one of the daughters of Agamemnon in the *Iliad*.

ITYS: Itys is the child of Philomela. See the entry for "Philomela."

LETO: the mother of Apollo and Artemis.

LIBYAN: somewhat vaguely defined area on the north shore of Africa, whose main Greek settlement was Cyrenaica. This region does not figure in Homer.

LYCIAN KING: See Apollo wolfkiller.

MAGNESIA: a region in Thessaly. It is mentioned here because the Magnesians and the Aenians are both mentioned in Homer's great catalogue of forces in book 2 of the *Iliad*.

MENELAUS: the brother of Agamemnon; the Trojan war was fought to regain his wife Helen after she had gone off with the Trojan prince, Paris.

MYCENAE: the traditional location of Agamemnon's palace, located on the northern edge of the plain known at the time of the play as Argos.

MYRTILUS: charioteer murdered by Pelops, ancestor of Agamemnon. See Pelops.

NEMESIS: the goddess who repays excessive acts.

NIGHTINGALE: See "Philomela."

NIOBE: Niobe (like Agamemnon in Electra's version of the sacrifice of Iphigenia) let fall an idle boast and Apollo and Artemis killed all of her children, and then was turned into a rock formation.

OLYMPUS: a mountain in northeastern Greece, the home of the gods.

ORESTES: the son of Agamemnon and Clytemnestra. In Aeschylus' *Oresteia*, he went to Athens and stood trial for murdering his mother, where he was acquitted. In Euripides' *Iphigenia in Tauris* we are told that these wanderings continued after the trial.

PELOPS: the son of Tantalus, came to the south of Greece (later to be called the Pelopon-nesos or island of Pelops) where he obtained his bride by winning a chariot race by bribing Myrtilus, the charioteer of her father. As payment for his service, Pelops murdered Myrtilus and threw him in the sea. Pelops was the father or grandfather of Atreus and Thyestes.

PERSEPHONE: queen of the dead.

PHANOTEUS: the ally of Clytemnestra and Aegisthus in Phocis.

PHILOMELA: Tereus married Philomela, and later raped her sister Procne. After murdering her child Itys to avenge her sister's rape, Philomela was turned into a nightingale, and she cries the name of her child "Itys" obsessively. Sophocles wrote a play (*Tereus*) about this murder and frequently refers to the nightingale in his plays. In some versions the names of the two sisters are reversed.

PHOCIS: the region in which Delphi is located.

PYLADES: the son of Strophius of Phocis and Orestes' partner in his adventures. In Aeschylus' *Oresteia* he makes a single short speech. He is a major character, however, in *Iphigenia in Tauris* and *Orestes* by Euripides.

PYTHO: another name for Delphi.

SPARTAN: Sparta is a city located in the Peloponnesos. In Homer it was the home of Menelaus, by reason of his marriage to Helen, whose father had been king there.

STROPHIUS: the ally of Orestes and Electra, and father of Pylades. He lives in Crisa.

THEMIS: a Titaness, who is associated with, and even stands for, law. Her name makes up the second half of the name of Chrysothemis.

THESSALIAN: Thessaly is a plain in northeastern Greece.

ZEUS: the king of the gods. The nightingale is called "the angel (i.e., messenger) of Zeus" in line 201. One explanation is that Zeus is the god in charge of the seasons (Horai) who are his daughters, and the nightingale announces the arrival of spring. However, the nightingale may be the "messenger of Zeus" for another reason. The nightingale mourns the death of a relative, as Electra does (1422–29), and so displays "the reverence / of Zeus (1465–66)."